AMAZON FBA AND PASSIVE INCOME IDEAS

2 BOOKS IN 1:

The Best Strategies and Secrets to Make Money From Home and Reach Financial Freedom - Amazon FBA, Dropshipping, Affiliate Marketing, Kindle Publishing, Blogging and More

Table of Contents

Amazon FBA 1

Introduction 5

Chapter 1: Get Started with Amazon FBA 13

Chapter 2: How to Have the Right Mindset 29

Chapter 3: How Amazon FBA Works 53

Chapter 4: Advantages and Disadvantages to Amazon FBA... 69

Chapter 5: Creating a Seller Account on Amazon ... 96

Chapter 6: Product Research 118

Chapter 7: Niche 140

Chapter 8: Suppliers 157

Chapter 9: How to Sell on Amazon 174

Chapter 10: Amazon Ads 194

Chapter 11: Creating Your Brand 215

Conclusion 223

References..232

Passive Income Ideas 2020 240

Introduction 244

Chapter 1: The Right Mind for Your Business 251

Chapter 2: Dropshipping 262

Chapter 3: Amazon FBA 277

Chapter 4: Affiliate Marketing 289

Chapter 5: Blogging 303

Chapter 6: Kindle Publishing 315

Chapter 7: Social Media Marketing 326

Chapter 8: Rental Income 337

Chapter 9: Cryptocurrency 347

Chapter 10: Google Adsense 356

Chapter 11: Online Courses 364

Chapter 12: AirBnB Business 374

Chapter 13: Dividend Investments 383

Chapter 14: Forex Trading 393

Chapter 15: Swing Trading 402

Chapter 16: Personal Brand 411

Chapter 17: Mobile App Development 420

Chapter 18: YouTube Videos 432

Chapter 19: Photography 444

Chapter 20: Mistakes to Avoid 452

Conclusion 457

References 462

Amazon FBA

The Ultimate Step-By-Step Guide for Beginners to Make Money Online from Home with Your E-Commerce Business by Selling on Amazon and Make Passive Income in 2020

Disclaimer Notice:

Please note the information contained within this document is for educational and entertainment purposes only. All effort has been executed to present accurate, up to date, and reliable, complete information. No warranties of any kind are declared or implied. Readers acknowledge that the author is not engaging in the rendering of legal, financial, medical or professional advice. The content within this book has been derived from various sources. Please consult a licensed professional before attempting any techniques outlined in this book.

By reading this document, the reader agrees that under no circumstances is the author responsible for any losses, direct or indirect, which are incurred as a result of the information contained within this document, including, but not limited to, — errors, omissions, or inaccuracies.

Introduction

What was one of the first things you wanted to sell when you were a kid? Did you have a lemonade stand that went bust after two weeks, or did you sell baseball bats at little league games? Whatever kickstarted your selling career shows the true determination of a natural-born seller that was meant to take advantage of one of the world's greatest merchandise companies: Amazon.

Amazon has been around for over 25 years, and it only continues to build momentum. Once marketed as only an online bookstore, it was unclear if the company would survive the next few years against such large alternatives such as Barnes & Noble. The company was completely internet-based, which many thought would be the end of the website, but it only became more popular with the addition of new products such as music and clothes.

Some may not realize that the company that started off as an internet-based store for books was one of the first platforms to encourage outside sales. Originally called zShops, people could market original work or hard-to-find items. The idea exploded as more than half a million people purchased something on Amazon by 2000. Jeff Bezos was dubbed the king of e-commerce in 2001, just seven years after Amazon's launch.

From its birth until now, Amazon has acquired 40 companies, but its major commerce is now in its third-party marketers. Outside sellers make up more than 50% of Amazon commerce today, and that number is only growing over the years. Online shopping has become the norm, and Amazon is leading the way in sales, accumulating billions of dollars every year, and its third-party sellers are riding the train to financial freedom.

Amazon FBA was officially launched in 2006, so it is far from the newest selling platform, but it has shaped the path for other platforms of its kind, and it should be considered as the best service possible. Sellers can use accounts created with Amazon to sell their own merchandise with small fees collected by Amazon. With the internet growing in importance every year, selling online has never been easier.

But why would you want to get involved with Amazon FBA? Well, if you have a knack for selling products, feel as though you have always wanted an online store, or just want to try something new, Amazon FBA is one of the easiest ways to get started. From its promises of prime delivery to customers to its total management of your products as soon as they are delivered to the warehouse, Amazon has you covered. They provide a service unmatched by any outside company, and they make selling easier every year.

There are thousands, if not millions, of sellers working with Amazon to sell the very best products, but just as many fail as succeed. That is a harsh statistic. However, that does not mean that you have to be one of the many who have failed. This book is designed to give you the best possible advice for creating your own Amazon shop and to succeed brilliantly.

So what causes some to succeed where others fail? A large part of the problem lies with the lack of information that many have when they start selling with Amazon FBA. They are unprepared to calculate the fees associated with an account, and worse yet, they start to sell blindly, hoping that they will eventually find a product that is worth the money and time. This type of randomized selling is what gets most sellers into trouble. Instead of researching their products to find better alternatives and provide the best products possible, they assume their products will sell themselves.

If you found a little bit of yourself in the last paragraph, do not worry. It is not uncommon to feel this way. When starting with Amazon, many get so excited that they forget there is a lot of hard work involved in becoming a successful entrepreneur, but it is not impossible. In fact, it is so possible that many people have quit their day jobs to just work at their Amazon business, making much more than they had before.

This book contains information about all fees associated with Amazon FBA and step-by-step guides to get you through the most difficult parts of research and selling. With this book, you will be able to navigate your way through the internet and find the right tools to make thoughtful and informed decisions about which products to buy and when to sell.

If you have never researched before, never fear. There are thousands of others who have been in the same boat as you, and they all learned to succeed. Much of the information that you find on the internet is either incorrect or will prevent you from selling as quickly as possible. *Amazon FBA: The Ultimate Step-By-Step Guide for Beginners to Make Money Online from Home with Your E-Commerce Business by Selling on Amazon and Make Passive Income in 2020* holds the tools necessary for you to start your business and thrive. This book has taken steps to make sure that you are provided with the best information possible to succeed.

This book includes the basics of Amazon and all the information you will need to set up an account, which includes giving you the right frame of mind to make the most of your situation and business. Starting a company takes as much mental work as it does physical work, and this book offers a guide to get you started.

Just like all good books, we want you to decide which is the best option for you, so we have created a comprehensive list that shows all the advantages and disadvantages of taking the plunge into Amazon FBA. With the best information possible, we want you to make the best decision for your future.

This book also walks you through the basics of starting an account and basic marketing. Do not worry if you find yourself anxious about any of these subjects. This step-by-step guide is designed to make marketing and research manageable, if not outright fun. With the information you need to find the right product, this book then guides you through selling with Amazon and how to get your foot in the door to make connections with companies that may change your life forever.

There has never been a better time to start with Amazon FBA. People from all over the world buy from Amazon, making it one of the biggest selling platforms in the world. People are always looking for the best new product and the most exciting finds, which is what you can bring to their lives. Hold no reservations when it comes to your Amazon FBA experience, and let us start the journey of a lifetime!

Chapter 1: Get Started with Amazon FBA

A common view of salespeople these days includes used car salesmen and those disgruntled employees as the local supermarket that just want to leave and be done with their job...permanently. However, the sales' playing field is changing considerably, and much of it can be done right from your home. Whether this is your first time selling anything or you've been doing low-key sales for years, Amazon FBA is an excellent place to start your career.

Think of the last time you could make a full living working less than eight hours each day. Likely, if you have been struggling with finances, you have not had a day off in months, and the 40-hour week is more like an 80-hour week. It is not uncommon to have multiple jobs to finance a family, but it does not have to be the only option. Amazon FBA does most of the work and expects only products from you. They handle the rest. Both you and Amazon gain income from each transaction, and the flat rates associated with Amazon FBA mean that there are no surprises.

What Is Amazon FBA?

Amazon Fulfillment By Amazon (FBA) has recently hit the lists as one of the most exciting ways to create your own business today, but it may surprise you to know that it has been around for quite some time. Since its origin in 2006, Amazon FBA has grown to influence one of the most basic business models for fulfillment, decimating the previous variable-fee platforms to create a basis for clean transactions with little to no surprises.

Amazon FBA takes the hassle out of creating shipping costs and delivery fees by creating a flat-rate system that has been adopted by companies seeking a competing background. Amazon FBA, however, holds the standard for this successful business model, and it is becoming increasingly easier for third-party members to become successful through this amazing program.

Amazon ships products using its Prime platform. If you are unfamiliar with Amazon Prime, it is a paid service that provides discounted items and free two-day shipping for all products that qualify. This means that every product that is shipped from Amazon is already available in warehouses across the United States, Canada, and Great Britain, though it offers shipping of products across the world. So, a product distributed to your local Amazon warehouse may reach people from all over the world.

Why Choose Amazon FBA?

There are many platforms available to sell products, including starting your own website. Amazon may hold the golden business standard for third-party manufacturers, but why should you get involved? If you want to get a product out into the market and have never started a business before, Amazon provides a platform to launch products on a website that is used by millions.

While it is true that Amazon sells by the billions every year, it is also one of the most competitive arenas in the merchant arena. However, this should not discourage you from taking a stab at creating a successful business with Amazon FBA. Many have found their calling simply by marketing products on social media for their Amazon stores. Before becoming a seller with

Amazon FBA, consider the statistics below to inspire your journey to an Amazon FBA career.

Most People Price Check with Amazon

Nine out of ten people searching for products on the internet eventually steer toward Amazon. Price-comparison sites often use Amazon as a top competitor to monitor changes in price, and it is easy to see why. Amazon offers fast, reliable service that is delivered promptly for all Amazon Prime members.

Because Amazon has become so trusted, many people opt for choosing Amazon over other similar sites. Not only do the prices affect the way many purchase, but the excellent customer service drives people back again and again.

Amazon's 350 Million Products

Amazon's excellent service and easy third-party access have provided an amazing platform for third-party sellers. Amazon's goal is to provide products for every occasion. Its mission statement is to provide everyone with the perfect products with the best service: "Our vision is to be Earth's most customer-centric company; to build a place where people can come to find and discover anything they might want to buy online" (as quoted from Dayton, 2019). Everyday items, such as home supplies, and unique products are all displayed on Amazon's website, available to anyone.

This may seem daunting for new Amazon sellers, but it does not mean that it is impossible to sell on Amazon. Competition is at an all-time high, so it is especially important to do research into your chosen field.

It is always good to know your market. When it comes to Amazon Prime, members are more likely to buy products than those who do not have an Amazon account. Why? The roughly $120 charged each year for the subscription comes with a number of perks including free two-day shipping on Prime products, access to entertainment such as movies and music, and early access to specific merchandise, just to name a few. Prime members are more aware of these products, as Amazon markets top items on its home page.

Members are also psychologically influenced by the great perks offered by Amazon Prime. Just as limited-time sales bring shoppers from all over to shop at a discounted price, Amazon Prime members also feel as though they need to take advantage of the perks that come with

Prime and spend more than those without memberships.

Since much of today's shopping is online, those who have access also like to take advantage of the free shipping. Items are more likely to sell online if customers can access the product with free shipping. Even if a product is listed as more on Amazon than another site that has paid shipping, shoppers will generally flock to Amazon, thinking they will receive a better deal.

With 95 million customers using Amazon Prime, the market for selling products has experienced exponential growth, and the new products added to inventory mean that the numbers will keep rising. Essentially, Amazon's large market has made it a hub for customer activity.

FBA Sellers See Up to Twice the Sales

Amazon Prime, the program responsible for the increase in sales in Amazon, is also the cause of the rise in revenue in FBA third-party sellers. Because people believe that they are receiving a deal by buying with Amazon Prime, average sales for third-party sellers increase dramatically. Coupled with two-day shipping, Amazon FBA merchants have the advantage of providing quality products that are more likely to sell.

Because the Amazon FBA draw is growing considerably, some products become overpopulated, and it is difficult to sell amidst the swarm of other deals. Creating a unique and useful product is the first step to creating a lasting career with Amazon FBA.

Around 50% of selling agents from Amazon are Amazon manufacturers. That means that roughly half of the merchants on Amazon are third-party sellers. This should come as no surprise since Amazon's FBA business started in 2006. Though there is a lot of competition to sell items on Amazon, it is also the perfect network to discover unique statistics for your shop.

Becoming a merchant with Amazon FBA is easy, and there are many resources for people who wish to hear success stories. The all-inclusive site promotes small businesses and provides a platform for successful businessmen and women to succeed.

The Selling Truth

There are many places to shop and to sell products. Think about the last time you went online to find something of value that required research, like a laptop. Did you go straight to Amazon or did you look around at Facebook Marketplace, eBay, or a company site? If you are a smart shopper, you likely looked around at different sites to determine the best price available and then made a decision based on quality and ratings. With so many other online shops that sell much of the same things, it is often difficult to choose which option is best.

eBay and Amazon are two of the leading companies that supply merchandise to the customer, so why choose Amazon over eBay? There are advantages and disadvantages for both, but when choosing the perfect site for your company from which your business can prosper, consider the results for both you and the customer.

eBay

As a platform with a high percentage of third-party sellers, eBay is often the first thought when selecting the perfect company for an online store. eBay customizes the selling experience for both the buyer and seller by offering bids when specified and creating a customized store. It offers many ways to sell products, giving the seller complete control over the availability of products and specifying shipping conditions.

eBay is primarily dependent on the seller. This means that the merchant must create the store, ship products, and create conditions upon returns. The rating system within eBay can also be considerably harsh. If the product is not shipped promptly or the seller does not provide top-tier customer service, ratings may significantly decrease the profit margins within eBay.

The time spent on products to create a large following within eBay requires a large chunk of the seller's time devoted to customer service. As the business grows, so does the responsibility for customer satisfaction. For small businesses that do not expect much deviation in products, eBay may be an excellent solution to selling, but rapidly growing businesses should seriously consider Amazon FBA.

Amazon FBA

Like eBay, Amazon has provided a platform that supports customers and sellers, but its commitment to both the customer and seller is unmatched in any other online store. Think about eBay as a stand at a farmer's market. All the people who come to buy products are guaranteed with satisfaction or their money back. The merchant must both create the products and provide the customer service required to bring people back again and again. Think of Amazon, however, as a shelf at the local grocery market. Shoppers must go through the store to find the product. The seller's job is only to provide the product, and the rest is processed through the grocery store.

Amazon creates time for sellers by giving them a place to store products that are sent from various warehouses across the world. Once the product is sent to Amazon, the company handles the shipping, customer service, and return policies, all for a flat rate. Time is one of the most important commodities in the business world, and Amazon gives sellers the opportunity to grow businesses without the hassle of losing time, keeping people happy.

Conclusion

Amazon Fulfillment By Amazon (FBA) is one of the best ways to sell products, and its easy-to-use portal and service make it one of the easiest ways to sell merchandise. Third-party sellers make up most of the merchants on the site, proof that the popular platform is one of the biggest draws for outside sellers.

Creating a seller account with Amazon FBA gives merchants larger opportunities to grow businesses. The large market and the unique items in Amazon make it the perfect place to advertise, and those who put forth the effort are likely to see large gains in profits.

Though Amazon has promised a wide range of products and a means by which to sell them, is it worth it to consider selling with Amazon FBA? That depends on how much drive you have for your business. Just like any small or large corporation, items are not going to sell on Amazon or anywhere else if the seller does not

put the time and energy into creating an
avenue for moving merchandise.

Chapter 2: How to Have the Right Mindset

You've no doubt heard that a successful business depends entirely on the effort one puts into the business. This is true for any other type of achievement. People who set their minds on achieving a goal are more likely to succeed than those who do not have a set plan.

That is easier said than done, however. The way to develop the right mindset is through creating a pliable response, which is known as a growth mindset. Whatever obstacles arise, the mind is capable of either making the logical solution far better or far worse than the situation warrants. Those who believe that they either do not deserve or cannot move on from a situation often feel repressed and cannot succeed. On the other hand, a growth mindset allows adaptivity to situations.

Consider when you were a child. Were you told that you were smart or that you could gain intelligence through hard work and study? Children who are told that they are smart become easily discouraged when they do not understand complicated material, exhibiting a closed mind. Children who are told they can learn through hard work and persistence are more adaptable.

When creating a business with Amazon's FBA program, consider the adaptability of your mind. If you believe that you can compete with others in the highly competitive world of Amazon FBA, you can. If you believe you cannot, you are right. A growth mindset allows for change and does not remain focused on small inconveniences. Selling on Amazon FBA requires a constant effort to market and improve upon products already released. To make a living with Amazon FBA, the products sent to Amazon must be of high enough caliber to encourage people to buy from your business again and again.

There are challenges, however, to developing a mindset that encourages you to set a high bar for your business. Without a growth mindset, small setbacks can seem difficult to overcome. To prevent slumps that lead to a lack of interest and action with your Amazon FBA business, take the time to research and start your business off with a bang.

Get Only the Best Information

With all of the information on the internet, it is often difficult to discern which information is helpful and which is not. It may surprise you to know that most of the information you can get on the internet is either not accurate or points you in the wrong direction. There are only some sites and blogs that offer true information that will help to grow your business.

The Good

Keep in mind that the best information to grow a business with Amazon FBA comes from the source: Amazon. Amazon has set up various web pages to help you find the correct information about Amazon FBA, including shipping costs and fees, how to set up an account, and more.

Find information from reputable sources such as books and selected blog articles. Books about making money through Amazon FBA, such as this one, are often thoroughly researched to provide the best information possible. They contain information about getting started and how to improve business. Books that rely on market research and show the best ways to maintain an active commission are the best to acquire. Blogs such as Money Nomad, Full-Time FBA, and JungleScout Blog are some of the best resources to find specialized and general information.

Become more acquainted with the market by doing research in your chosen field. General knowledge of Amazon FBA is important, but knowing the market for the products you sell is essential. Every niche is different, so discover articles and books related to your product. The more you know about it, the easier it becomes to sell the product.

For example, marketing for a hula hoop is going to look different than marketing for an iPhone. Select the market that frequently searches for your product. Many markets may look for a hula hoop, but what makes yours different from the rest? Does it sparkle? Does it have lights? Information regarding what the market would want in a hula hoop is available online, and knowing what the customers want in a product will earn you a profit.

The Bad

As mentioned previously, most of the resources on the internet are not helpful in developing a business. A Google search may yield millions of results, but they are often unimpressive and incorrect. It takes time to sift through all of the less-helpful information, so as a general rule, avoid novelty blogs, promotions, and paid training. Though training may be beneficial to start with Amazon FBA, most are either scams or hold too much information that can only be accessed once.

Ads that are common on sites such as Facebook and Instagram are often wrong or lack key elements to starting a successful business unless you pay a large amount of money. Any subscriptions offered through social media or ineffectual media sites should be avoided. They often oversaturate emails with useless information, wasting time that should be spent on developing products and marketing.

Make Role Models of the Best Sellers

One of the best ways to create a successful business is to research the works of others. After all, the luxuries seen today are developed through research and improvement on the works of others. Follow instructions and generate ideas through careful study of best practices.

People who have grown successful businesses are great role models, and with the information on the internet, it is often possible to follow their steps to creating a lasting career with Amazon FBA. A great way to start is to research people who have used a style like your own to build businesses. People such as Steve Jobs and Bill Gates are common examples of people who have worked toward a goal and have achieved success. Books about successful people let you know how to find your place in the business world and are often the blueprints for success.

Becoming an Amazon FBA seller requires knowledge of the market, as mentioned previously. However, doing research on Amazon FBA sellers who have marketed and sold products similar to yours provides an in-depth analysis of what you need the most: a way to reach your audience. It is wise to avoid people who offer training at a price because free resources often hold the best information.

Create a Vision

Beliefs are the foundations for all actions in life. If you believe you can, you are right, and if you believe you cannot, you are right. Many believe that they cannot create a future while creating a web of excuse after excuse after excuse. The lies you tell yourself come true, and it is important to understand that beliefs are not reality.

Though beliefs change the reality around you, they do not define facts nor your future. For example, many believed that vaccines caused autism based on a fabricated study that has been disproven many times over. However, because people believed that vaccines were the cause of brain malfunctions, they passed on fabricated knowledge to people today. That belief has defined the reality of many, but it is not supported by facts.

Just as the belief that vaccines cause autism became a life-altering belief, so can destructive beliefs cause failure in your life. These limiting beliefs cause failure, not the statistics that guide the success of your business. Instead of submitting yourself to false beliefs, take a moment to criticize the beliefs that you hold. Examine your beliefs and discover what drives you and what hinders you.

Consider your beliefs. When it comes to selling on Amazon FBA, how do you view success? Are you only interested in a general scheme to sell merchandise, or are you considering the niche, market, cost, and reward? Creating a vision for your future business provides a pathway for future growth and development. Discover what you envision your business to be by laying down a plan to complete your goal.

Your greatest enemy when trying to complete your goals is you. Think about it. When was the last time that you accomplished a goal that you believed was impossible to reach? The only way to achieve a goal is by believing that you can succeed. This includes the necessity for frequent reality checks. How far have you come from the start of your business, and what mistakes have you made?

Though challenging, changing your belief system from one of success that is dependent on frequent success to one that accepts small mistakes is the first step to creating a successful business. Change the way you think about success by asking yourself the following questions:

- How can I view money in a way that will profit myself and those who work for me?
- What can I change to feel as though mistakes are simple consequences of hard work?

- How can I develop my skills to better serve myself and my customers?
- What can I do to experience the fruits of my labor?

Simple affirmations with a focus on how you can change your life to profit yourself and others help you stay on the right track and creates a goal that is easy to follow.

Set Goals

People who are successful take the time to set goals. Creating time frames for the completion of tasks that range from short-term to long-term keeps you focused on the importance of your future. But how do you set goals that will benefit both you and the company you are trying to create?

Successful goals are developed through the SMART goal system. Though it has now been around for many years, it is a good place to start when considering how to develop short- and long-term goals for the future. SMART stands for Specific, Measurable, Assignable, Realistic, and Time-Oriented.

Consider setting up your first sale through Amazon FBA. The sale must include a variety of extra tasks like finding your niche, paying for materials, retrieving materials, assembling materials, sending them to Amazon, marketing, and creating a system to automate your business. Any one of these is an example of a small goal that can fulfill the SMART goal system, but we will just focus on finding your niche in this example. The first step to completing the goal is to write it down by completing the SMART acronym.

S-Specific: Keep a goal specific by narrowing down your search with research. To sell on Amazon FBA, research the niche in which you want to sell and build on it. For example, the niche could be luxury towels, dog beds, or heaters. Within these groups, break down the information further by researching the best brands, quality reviews, and uses. You might even find that you will break down your search even more than you originally thought.

M-Measurable: Any goal must be measurable; success is measured. To create a goal that will stand the test of time, break it down into parts that will help you achieve your goal. For example, if you sell heaters, you will need to know the price of each unit, its shipping expectation, and its specifications, just to name a few. Research how much money it will take to get you started and set each goal accordingly.

A-Attainable: What is attainable for you may be unattainable for others. Likewise, while others might boast thousands of sales each month, you may only realistically be able to sell 25 units. The goal you set for yourself should push you toward a higher end goal, but it should not be out of reach. Creating an attainable goal means giving yourself the time and patience to achieve the goal. Without attainable goals, you will surely sink into a pit of frustration that is difficult to overcome.

R-Realistic: Though setting large goals is recommended, setting large, unrealistic goals prevents goal completion. Think about selling with Amazon FBA. If your goal is to sell one million products by the end of the first year, it is time to take a step back. Though it is certainly possible to do this, it is incredibly difficult, and setting such an unrealistic goal can cause frustration. Instead, break down goals into reasonable chunks. For example, if you are just starting with Amazon FBA, consider a realistic number of heaters you may sell. For the first month, set a goal to sell 25. At the end of the month, analyze your results and set a new goal for the future. Relying on statistics and past experience is essential to create a basis for new goals.

T-Time-Oriented: Consider a goal to sell one million products with Amazon FBA, but you do not include a time limit on this request. Frankly, it is unlikely to get done. Goals that have time limits not only help you envision your future, but they also inspire you to reach those goals by any means necessary. Selling one million products with Amazon FBA is a great end goal, but it is ultimately more helpful to divide the tasks into smaller goals. For example, give yourself time to sell your first few products. Find a groove that works for you and then base larger goals on data from the successes of smaller goals.

Find Your Brand

Developing your voice within the Amazon FBA community depends on how you wish to present yourself. For example, if you are looking to create a connection with single mothers, find the best products that will encourage them to buy. The voice you create within your business is the brand that will stick with you for years.

Your target audience is important to building your brand, and the way to stay motivated when selling to this market is to have a vested interest in its success. For example, if you are someone who sits in an office all day with little to no change in pace, you may consider selling exercise equipment that is useful when sitting all day. This market has a background that is similar to yours, and you will better understand the audience, bringing in more sales.

Create a mission statement that will determine how you intend to improve the lives of your customers. Mission statements keep you focused and drive you to improve. The more value you place upon your company, the more others will place, as well. They will expect service that is on par with the rest of your merchandise. Include in your mission statement the goals you wish to achieve and provide your own brand of motivation you can review whenever you need a boost.

Creating a list that discusses the benefits and key factors of your company is also a great way to build your brand. It is not easy to sell a product for which you have no love. Since this is your business and not one in which you are simply employed, take pride in your products. What makes your brand better than those around you? How does your service compare to competitors'? Though Amazon handles much of the customer service, keep in mind that it is up to you to market your products, so quick responses should be at the top of your priority list.

Find your voice with your company by exploring how you want to sell and to whom. For example, consider the voice of someone selling textbooks to a university. Likely, universities will be concerned with the material within and the ease of understanding. Now consider someone selling textbooks to a family. The family may also be looking for ease of understanding, but they may also be concerned with the applicability of the material, or they might wonder why they should buy textbooks in the first place. The way each is sold is completely unique, so discover what voice is unique to you and play upon your strengths.

Since you are unique, your company should be unique as well. Develop a brand with personality, and follow through on creative ideas. Customers who come back again and again often look at the creativity of marketing. Personalize each sale with subsequent thanks for the sales.

While finding a voice for your products and business, always be the first to advocate for your brand. Take pride in your business and promote your best work. Remember that you are the one responsible for bringing customers to your products, so do not be afraid of taking on the extra work to make your products shine. Constantly consider how to improve your business and remember to let others know how important your products really are.

Consistency, Consistency, Consistency

The only way to be successful in any industry is through consistency. If you are not seeing the sales you prefer, step up your game in marketing. If you are not receiving the products you sent out for, follow up and set up schedules to track your inventory. Consistency means finding ways to improve and following through on the menial tasks.

It is no secret that those who "keep at it" often develop their businesses quicker and see more success than those who do work irregularly. Using the motivational advice above, find a reason to want to sell, and building your business will become easier all the time. Develop a love for your products and provide a reason for your customers to love them as well.

Conclusion

Creating a growth mindset is important in building a business. When you allow yourself to see the mistakes made and prevent yourself from delving too deeply into frustration, you will see your perspective change rapidly. The only way to develop and change your mindset is through persistent devotion to yourself and your work.

The good information gleaned from the internet and books helps to create motivation when seeing the successes of others. A successful business through Amazon FBA is possible, and the best sources will let you know how to get there. Beware, however, of the bad information. Many blogs and forums on the internet are often steeped with bad advice that prevents success.

Find the best role models for your business by selecting those who have succeeded in a wide variety of subjects. They often pass along valuable information that is important to success. Develop a daily ritual to spend time in a book every day to gain more knowledge about their lives and build a strong background for yourself.

Beliefs that are destructive often make entrepreneurs feel as though they cannot achieve goals. Incorrect beliefs, such as those that cause frustration, are toxic, so develop a healthy relationship with your brain by giving yourself a pat on the back. The goals you achieve are necessary to keep consistent and realistic beliefs. Build practical goals that will encourage you to succeed.

Your brand is what people will remember when they buy your products. Often, when you give a valuable product, customers will look for your brand again to buy more. Never underestimate the importance of consistently keeping up with customers. People who respect your brand will expect consistent marketing and will build a solid relationship with your business.

Chapter 3: How Amazon FBA Works

Now that you have been properly motivated, how does Amazon FBA work? Amazon has been set up to create a business platform that is convenient for both the customer and the seller. Because of this, selling with Amazon FBA has never been easier, and when you have become used to the way the process works, you can set up an automated solution to basic selling.

How It Works

Many platforms today work with both the seller and customer to create the ultimate shopping experience. Luckily, Amazon's process for selling has been refined to provide easy access to third-party sellers. The majority of the work is done by Amazon, and you are responsible for getting products sent to its warehouses. All of the basics for Amazon FBA are broken down into easy-to-follow steps.

Send Your Products to Amazon

Though Amazon is known for its wide storage of items, it cannot sell your products if you do not send them to Amazon and set up the store with your Amazon FBA account. Amazon is in charge of holding your products, but you must act as any other online store and create a way for the products to sell.

Products sent to Amazon must be stored in one of the many warehouses in the United States, Canada, and Great Britain. Before you start listing and selling your products, you need to determine how much shipping will cost in the future. Changing the price of your products is discouraged, and fiddling around with prices due to the change of shipping information may hurt your online shop.

If you have a website already set up for your business (as many third-party sellers do), you will no doubt recognize the steps to creating a successful business. All information regarding your products should be listed with the product. Many people want to buy products that have a rich history or have significant information. Remember, if you do not have any reviews for your products, the best way to secure future buyers is to provide information they can use.

Amazon Stores Your Product

Inventory that Amazon receives from third-party sellers is categorized and placed in an organized fashion. They distribute packages according to size, packing labels, and weight. Some of Amazon FBA's fees are associated with the storage of your products in their warehouses. Think of it as renting a space in a large store. You will have the benefit of their client base, but you still need to give some reason for the merchandise to stay.

The fees for storing products depend largely on the weight, and each package is categorized in standard or oversized package sizes. The weights and prices are listed in Table 3.1 and Table 3.2 below.

Table 3.1: Fees for standard products with Amazon FBA.

AMAZON FBA STANDARD FEES				
	Small Standard	Large Standard	Larger Standard	Largest Standard
Weight	< 12 oz.	12 oz. to 1 lb.	1 lb. to 2 lb.	2 lb. to 20 lb.
FBA Fee	$2.41	$3.19	$4.71	$4.71 + $0.38 per lb. over 2 lb.

Table 3.2: Fees for oversized products with Amazon

AMAZON FBA OVERSIZE FEES				
	Small Oversize	Medium Oversize	Large Oversize	Special Oversize
Weight	20 lb. to 70 lb.	70 lb. to 150 lb.	70 b. to 150 lb.	>150 lb.
Long Side + Girth	< 130 in.	< 130 in.	< 165 in.	>165 in.
FBA Fee	$8.13 + $0.38 per lb. over 2 lb.	$9.44 + $0.39 per lb. over 2 lb.	$75.78 + $0.79 per lb. over first 90 lbs.	$137.32 + $0.91 per lb. over first 90 lbs.

As expected, the larger the weight, the bigger the fee to store your products, so plan accordingly. You are in charge of keeping all products in stock. Amazon does not poke and prod you to keep your inventory active and available. You must keep track of all products sent to Amazon.

Along with initial storage fees, Amazon also requires a monthly payment for products stored. However, these are usually not unreasonable. They are subcategorized into the months required for holding the products. January through September, for example, are cheaper monthly than October through December. Table 3.3 displays these costs.

Table 3.3: Amazon FBA monthly storage fees.

MONTHLY AMAZON FBA FEES		
Month	Standard Products	Oversize Products
January – September	$0.69 per cubic ft.	$0.48 per cubic ft.
October – December	$2.40 per cubic ft.	$1.20 per cubic ft.

When a customer buys your product, Amazon works as the middleman and ships your product for you with no additional cost to you. Your inventory will likewise reflect the changes made with recent purchases.

Amazon Ships Your Product

Amazon's famous Prime shipping means that the customer will receive the product in one to two days. Since the product is out of your hands, you no longer need to worry about the shipping. All products shipped with Amazon are delivered through large shipping companies such as UPS. All you need to do now is wait for the money to come in.

Amazon Handles Customer Service

To those who are afraid to use phones, it should come as a huge relief that Amazon handles customer service...at least most of it. Amazon has developed long relationships with their customers. They follow up on products sold and make sure the product was received and is in good condition. They are also responsible for answering any questions related to the product, and they handle reviews.

That takes a lot of pressure off of you, but you are still responsible for some of the customer service work. Just as with any company, in order to grow your stock and retain customers, you need to seek ways to improve your work. The feedback you receive from customers is of the utmost importance to building an empire with Amazon FBA. It is your responsibility to keep customers satisfied with your products and offer new, innovative ways to improve.

You Get Paid

Some of the best words in the English language are the words "you get paid." As a reward for your hard work, you receive payments for the products sold. Everything in the transaction is handled by Amazon, and every two weeks, they deduct the fees associated with your account and hand you a large payout.

The fees associated with working with Amazon FBA are not often the first thought when receiving a payout, so it is important to understand that there are several fees associated.

Referral Fees: Amazon keeps some of the profit made from a sold product since they do most of the work. Referral fees differ for many products and are usually higher for items with the Amazon brand. For example, Kindles and Amazon Echoes are among the highest for referral fees. Amazon takes approximately 45% of the profit. However, for items not associated with Amazon, the percentages are much smaller. Items such as books and electronics usually do not exceed a 20% referral fee.

Variable Closing Fees: Though rarer than most fees, variable closing fees are flat fees that correspond to products such as books and DVDs. Be sure to research how much these fees will cost when deciding on a product to sell with Amazon FBA.

FBA Fees: Along with all the other fees, it should come as no surprise that Amazon charges an FBA fee that comes with selling products on their site. The fee goes toward selling and shipping your product, and in the long run, it is actually less expensive than packing and shipping the items yourself. In the end, the price for all the work that Amazon FBA does for you is just a few dollars. That is quite a deal.

Individual Seller Fees: There are two types of sales accounts of which we will discuss in greater detail in later chapters. Individual sellers do not have a subscription with Amazon FBA and pay $1.00 as a flat charge for any product sold.

Subscription Seller Fees: Subscription sellers are people who do a lot of selling on Amazon FBA. The fee to subscribe to Amazon FBA is $39.99 per month. That may seem like a lot, but if you are selling large quantities of products, this is the route to take. Instead of the flat individual seller fee, Amazon charges a monthly subscription that does not take out any additional fees for products sold. If you are selling more than 40 products each month, it is best to set up a subscription.

What You Do

So much of Amazon FBA is handled by Amazon professionals, so you do not have to worry about much of the heavy lifting. However, the work that you put into your business is the most important. It is up to you to supply products, keep the inventory in stock, and advertise for your company. Never think that simply sending in your products is the end of the road. There is a lot of work left to do to have a successful business.

Choose Products

Though the majority of strategies for choosing products is discussed in later chapters, it is important to briefly discuss it here. You are responsible for providing a product that others are likely to buy. Though it may seem like a successful venture to blow all your money on hippo decorations, you must realize that this market is very small. Hippo collectors may feel ecstatic to see your inventory, but it is unlikely they will see your product line if you do not know which markets to hit.

When choosing products, decide on a final product that makes you happy. That may seem corny, but it will actually help you market your products more effectively. Think about it. The love you have for a product will translate to your shoppers if you put in enough effort.

Keep Inventory in Stock

The inventory you put on Amazon needs to be continually stocked. If you plan on creating a product yourself, consider how many you will need to keep your business afloat. Customers that value your product also value its availability. Consider the last time you went shopping at your favorite store. Even if you went into the store with the expectation of buying only one thing, it is more than possible that you exited the store with more than you thought.

Impulse buying is one of the best ways to catch a customer's attention. When looking for a sweater for a niece or nephew, a customer might just come across your store of raven-themed miniatures. Often mistaking cuteness for class, the customer may think this is the perfect addition to the birthday box. However, if an item is frequently out of stock, customers lose interest and forget your product.

When selling items in many sizes and colors, always create a store that can supply at least twice what you think will sell. For example, if you create rings and sell them with Amazon FBA, do research about the most common ring size, the most popular colors for the season, and keep a supply handy. Sending just one of every style may create a "limited time only" sensation, but it will hardly encourage people to find your products in the future.

Market and Advertise

Like choosing products, this subject will be covered in more detail in chapters 9 and 10. However, before you even set up an account with Amazon FBA, consider the marketing that you can do for your product. Perform research about your chosen product, and develop a strategy that will bring in the right audiences.

Conclusion

The bulk of work to do with Amazon FBA comes from Amazon's end, which is highly beneficial to you. It allows you the time you need for creating and marketing for your products.

Once you have set up your store, send your products to Amazon through either Amazon's service or a common carrier like FedEx, UPS, or the USPS. Remember that the more reliable the shipping service you have, the more likely it is that your inventory will have a steady flow of products. Once Amazon receives your product, the product itself is out of your hands. Amazon handles the storage, shipping, and customer service that comes with the sold product. You get to reap the rewards of supplying products to Amazon without the hassle of dealing with customers.

When the inventory is out of your hands, your job is not done. Instead, you must still keep your business stocked with products. That includes regular shipping to Amazon and constant market research. To get the most out of your shop, you must know your audience and how they respond to different stimuli. Be involved with your customers. Be sure to answer any questions quickly and set up a rapport with faithful clients.

Chapter 4: Advantages and Disadvantages to Amazon FBA

Just as with any other company, Amazon FBA has many advantages and disadvantages. Be informed about your decision to set up a business with Amazon FBA by being aware of how each part of the company can affect your business.

Most businesses use Amazon FBA in conjunction with their own websites, and this is often because the business and exposure they get from Amazon FBA translates into their outside businesses. It is wise to have a stake in both a personal website and Amazon FBA account, though we will not go into further detail here. Suffice it to say that, before you fully commit yourself to selling on Amazon full-time, consider these advantages and disadvantages.

Advantages

One of the largest advantages of Amazon FBA is its accessibility. That means that anyone can access Amazon and select your products without fear of running into scams or internet viruses. Along with its highly marketable platform, Amazon also works with you as a seller to create products that are better for you and your customers. These, among many other reasons, are why many people opt for a business with Amazon FBA.

When considering the advantages of any venture, always consider how well you will profit from the collaboration. Below are more examples of Amazon's excellent service and the advantages that come with becoming an Amazon FBA seller.

Logistics and Shipping

Even if you have never owned a store before, you have likely experienced the grueling sluggishness and painstaking process that is mail delivery. Little inconveniences like the wrong stamps or the incorrect weight of a package can prevent you from making deliveries on time, and busy times, such as those around the holidays, can slow your business to a stop while you try to keep up with the demand.

When sending packages for your own business, you have to think about how quickly your shipping will reach the customer and what rating you will receive if a package is late. Often, when products get lost in the mail or delivery is delayed, you are the one that receives the brunt of a customer's wrath. The logistics with shipping packages can become exceptionally difficult to maintain, and if you are not experienced with shipping packages, some items may not be sent at all.

When you are part of the Amazon FBA family, you no longer have to worry about shipping or the logistics that come from untimely package delivery. Amazon has shipped billions of products, so they know the procedure. Also, if a product is lost in the mail, Amazon will take care of the customer for you, giving you an extra payment for the merchandise lost.

Discounted Shipping Rates

Not only does Amazon handle the shipping of new products, but it also provides both customer and seller with major discounts. The major mail delivery companies that work with Amazon offer major discounts because of the many packages they deliver. This means that both customers and sellers profit from the discounts.

Packages sent to Amazon in accord with Amazon FBA receive these discounts. Also, the two-day shipping that Amazon gives all Prime customers is a huge draw for customers. Those who come for the products may stay for the shipping. Its service is among the only of its kind. Shoppers with Amazon Prime subscriptions are more likely to shop, making your product line more accessible than ever.

Management of Returns

Returns are one of the most obnoxious parts of owning a business. Businessmen and women often have to shoulder the responsibility of paying for return shipping, refunds, and the cost it takes to send a new product, if you are lucky.

You may be surprised to know that returns are more common than you would expect. Clothing is often returned because online fitting is difficult. With Amazon's Prime Wardrobe, they handle returns often, as customers can send back clothing that does not fit or work for them. People also commonly return items that are broken or otherwise impaired. If a large chunk of your inventory has the same defect, the number of customers that return merchandise can explode.

Luckily, Amazon takes care of the dirty work for you when you sign up for Amazon FBA. The return shipping Amazon provides makes the task quick and easy, and you will see the changes to your store when the items are returned. Again, products are returned directly to Amazon, so you do not need to worry about additional shipping.

There is, however, a price to pay with return shipping. Amazon generally charges a fee every time a product is returned. The return fee is equal to the fulfillment fee, which you can calculate from Tables 3.1 and 3.2. Though that might seem like a pain, consider the advantages. Customer loyalty grows when they are offered free products or services, and free return shipping drives many shoppers to purchase merchandise on Amazon. When it comes down to the financials, letting Amazon take care of your returns really adds up in the bank. You will likely see a profit increase due to the number of products you are able to send in.

Customer Service Management

Dealing with customers is one of the leading causes of quitting jobs. Customers can be difficult to rein in when they have complaints, and it can become extremely discouraging to deal with people who do not like your product. Coupled with multiple returns, owning a business may not seem like the dream you believed it to be after all.

Amazon is one of the best customer service providers in the world. They have to be to get customers returning again and again. When you do not have to spend hours on the phone explaining why an order is not satisfactory, why not leave it to the professionals? With Amazon FBA, customers with complaints take their grievances directly to Amazon instead of bothering you.

Unlimited Storage Space

When developing an empire, storage space is one of the top necessities to keep your business running smoothly. Consider becoming a DVD or Blu-ray distributor, and your products are extremely popular due to the popularity of a recently released movie. To keep up with demand, you would need to either buy or rent a storage facility to take care of all your inventory. The costs for maintaining this storage facility may start to wipe you out, and understandably so. The more inventory you acquire, the greater the chance you have to make a profit, but it comes at a storage price.

Amazon has over 175 warehouses with over 150 million square feet to store your products (Amazon, n.d.). The only requirements to fulfill when storing products in the Amazon warehouses are listed in Table 3.3. Though there are fees associated with keeping products stored there, the price is far below what it would cost to rent a warehouse of your own.

Unlimited storage space is available for Amazon FBA sellers that are top in their class. Effectively, this means that if you are a high-profile seller with a high performance score, you can provide Amazon with as many products as you want. This cost-efficient approach makes it easier for top sellers to maintain high statuses.

Quick Delivery

As with all Prime-eligible products, shipping is free and sends within two days. The faster products make it to your customers, the more likely they are to buy from your store again. Customers come to expect fast shipping, so shipping with Amazon ensures that you will be on top of the game.

Quick delivery has advantages for sellers in other ways as well. For instance, since products sent to Amazon with the Amazon FBA program receive discounted shipping costs, sellers can quickly stock inventory if the supply is low. If you are new to the business and do not know how much inventory to send to Amazon, the quick delivery to Amazon can get you out of a pinch.

Amazon's Multi-Channel Fulfillment (MCF)

Though commonly confused with Amazon FBA, Amazon's Multi-Channel Fulfillment uses Amazon to store products but send via third-party sites. For example, many FBA sellers have a website outside of Amazon; in fact, 80% of sellers do. This means that they are getting business from another site. Using the same principles as Amazon FBA, sellers that utilize MCF send all their products to Amazon who stores and distributes products, but all is done through personal business channels.

MCF is entirely dependent on outside sources. MCF users often use other selling sites to promote and sell merchandise; eBay is a common platform for MCF use. Sellers build loyalty with customers by offering the same shipping and service requirements that Amazon has, but merchants are not responsible for what happens to the product after it arrives at the Amazon facility.

The fees for MCF are slightly different than for those expressly interested in Amazon FBA.

Standard-Size Products (Per Unit)					
Size	1 Unit Order	2 Unit Order	3 Unit Order	4 Unit Order	5 + Unit Order
Standard 3-5 Business Day Shipping					
Small: < 1 lb.	$5.85	$3.75	$3.35	$3.25	$2.20
Large: < 1 lb.	$5.90	$3.90	$3.40	$3.30	$2.80
Large: 1 – 2 lb.	$5.95	$3.95	$3.45	$3.35	$2.95
Large: > 2 lb.	$5.95 + $0.39/lb.	$3.95 + $0.39/lb.	$3.45 + $0.39/lb.	$3.35 + $0.39/lb.	$2.95 + $0.39/lb.
Expedited 2 Day Shipping					
Small: < 1 lb.	$7.90	$4.65	$3.55	$3.40	$2.41
Large: < 1 lb.	$8.30	$4.80	$3.80	$3.55	$2.99
Large: 1 – 2 lb.	$8.35	$5.35	$5.15	$4.95	$4.18
Large: > 2 lb.	$8.35 + $0.39/lb.	$5.35 + $0.39/lb.	$5.15 + $0.39/lb.	$4.95 + $0.39/lb.	$4.18 + $0.39/lb.
Priority Next Day Shipping					
Small: < 1 lb.	$12.80	$7.30	$6.30	$5.80	$4.30
Large: < 1 lb.	$13.80	$7.80	$6.80	$5.90	$4.80
Large: 1 – 2 lb.	$13.85	$7.85	$6.85	$5.95	$4.85
Large: > 2 lb.	$13.85 + $0.39/lb.	$7.85 + $0.39/lb.	$6.85 + $0.39/lb.	$5.95 + $0.39/lb.	$4.85 + $0.39/lb.

Table 4.1: Displays standard shipping prices for MCF users.

Tables 4.1 and 4.2 display the fees associated with Amazon's MCF.

Table 4.2: Amazon shipping prices for oversized packages. Information retrieved from Ama

OVERSIZE PRODUCTS (PER UNIT)					
Size	1 Unit Order	2 Unit Order	3 Unit Order	4 Unit Order	5 + Unit Order
Standard 3 – 5 Business Day Shipping					
Small: > 2 lb.	$12.30 + $0.39/lb.	$6.80 + $0.39/lb.	$5.80 + $0.39/lb.	$4.80 + $0.39/lb.	$3.80 + $0.39/lb.
Medium: > 2 lb.	$15.30 + $0.39/lb.				
Large: > 90 lb.	$78.30 + $0.80/lb.				
Special: > 90 lb.	$143.30 + $0.92/lb.				
Expedited 2 Day Shipping					
Small: > 2 lb.	$13.30 + $0.39/lb.	$7.80 + $0.39/lb.	$7.30 + $0.39/lb.	$7.15 + $0.39/lb.	$6.85 + $0.39/lb.
Medium: > 2 lb.	$16.80 + $0.39/lb.				
Large: > 90 lb.	$78.30 + $0.80/lb.				
Special: > 90 lb.	$143.30 + $0.92/lb.				
Priority Next Day Shipping					
Small: < 1 lb.	$20.80 + $0.39/lb.	$11.30 + $0.39/lb.	$8.20 + $0.39/lb.	$7.70 + $0.39/lb.	$7.30 + $0.39/lb.
Large: < 1 lb.	$31.30 + $0.39/lb.				
Large: 1 – 2 lb.	$78.30 + $0.80/lb.				
Large: > 2 lb.	$143.30 + $0.92/lb.				

Disadvantages

Though Amazon FBA has multiple benefits and advantages, it would not be a true company if it did not have its own rules. The disadvantages associated with Amazon FBA are often included with the advantages. Though there are wonderful perks, many come at a price. The only way to determine if selling with Amazon FBA is the right fit for you is to weigh the advantages and disadvantages.

Fees and Costs

We have already discussed a majority of the fees associated with Amazon FBA, but there are others that affect overall profit within the platform. If products stay in Amazon warehouses instead of selling, they will ultimately cost you a bundle in sky-high costs.

Have you ever wondered how some people can afford the prices at which they sell their products? Some merchandise on Amazon sells for only $2.00, way below what most would believe is a success. In this case, most people would be right. People cannot earn a profit on Amazon by selling products at extraordinarily low prices. While it may seem as though selling thousands of T-shirts at $2.50 each will pay off in the long run, many fail to realize not only the basic fees but also those that are buried under a long page of script.

Amazon has provided businesspeople with a calculator that will determine all fees associated with their products. However, many of these fees are estimated, and you may not always receive a clear picture of the charges. When determining what products to sell and how many, always round up. Even if you will not have to pay the higher prices, this will give you the maximum rate at which to sell products.

Storage fees may also seem like a small price to pay for signing up with one of the greatest selling platforms in the world, but consider how these fees can build up over time. For instance, if you sell miniature lizards that weigh approximately 2 oz., you may believe that the deal you get from storing them on Amazon far outweighs the small costs of storage. However, if you believe that your porcelain lizards will be the hit of the decade and you send 1,000 figurines to Amazon, the price for storing your merchandise really starts to stack up. Even with the smallest weight class, it will cost you $690 each month to store your lizards, which only includes the months of January to September. As the holidays roll around, you will be paying $2,400 each month just for the storage.

Many people blindly start selling with Amazon FBA without doing research. Amazon FBA could seem like a rip-off if you are not careful about your products and market research. To prevent throwing away your money, take care of your inventory and keep an eye on marketing successes.

More Frequent Returns

Maintaining a strict policy on your website may prevent people from buying from your store, but offering fast and free returns increases the likelihood of more frequent returns. Since Amazon is known for its impeccable customer service, people are more likely to flock to the easy returns.

What does this mean for you? First, you will suffer the loss of a product that has not been sold, and you may have to continue to pay for its storage fees over time. Since you are charged for every return, the price for easier customer shipping also means that you are not seeing the same returns. If you are marketing a product that has size variations or inadequacies, you may see return fees build up quickly.

Difficult Product Prep

Though Amazon takes the guesswork out of handling products once they are received into warehouses, it does have rather strict guidelines for sending the merchandise. Any product that is not correctly labeled or sent to the right facility may be sent back at the seller's expense.

Trouble Tracking Inventory

When you run your own business, you can keep track of all inventory in and out of the shop. Receipts and order slips remind you who purchased what. Returns are handled by yourself or employees who know information about the customer, such as a phone number, email address, or the last four digits of a credit card. Shops that are run internally are designed to keep customer information for subsequent payments and to be a more personalized shop. It is not uncommon for a small business to know many of his or her customers by name.

Amazon FBA tracking, however, makes these connections much more difficult because, like most online stores, it does all of the above tracking for you. Much of your time as an Amazon FBA merchant is spent worrying about the products in terms of creating, shipping, packing, and making improvements. Though you may receive information from Amazon regarding product reviews, much of the personality of your business is exchanged for convenience.

It is not required to know the names of your customers, but when it comes to tracking packages, additional information is helpful for keeping track of orders. Amazon offers tools to make tracking easier, but it is still difficult to keep a handle on which orders went where and which customer left what review. If only one item was damaged, you may have to wade through multiple reviews to offer refunds or ask for product improvement, which takes a lot of precious time.

Difficult Sales Taxes

Keeping track of taxes can seem overwhelming for the smallest of businesses, but calculating tax with Amazon can become an absolute nightmare without help. Since Amazon is based in different states and countries, taxes vary. Even more frustrating, Amazon frequently moves products to different warehouses, changing the taxes on the products sold. Passing the road signs to even more complicated ground, you have to consider sales *and* shipping taxes. These also vary per state, and they might feel difficult to track with the range of different purchases.

Sales tax does not belong to the seller. Instead, the money collected from the tax goes directly to the states in which it is requested. But how do you keep track of which states need so much money? Amazon collects taxes for each state, but they do not give a clear pathway to set up payments to these states.

Various tools are set up to help you pay the right taxes for every state or country in which you do business. Amazon has its own section in sellers' FBA accounts that shows what the taxes are for the states in which you sold merchandise. Unfortunately, you will either have to be an accountant or have access to software that will help you sort out all tax information and lay it out in a readable form.

Commingling

Commingling with Amazon FBA allows you to bunch your products with other sellers'. When you see a product on Amazon, often there are buying options that allow you to select from which seller to buy. People from all over the globe can add to a single product, often providing a large selection of products. Commingling can offer you more contact with your product, but there are problems with this system that can lead to serious charges held against you and anyone else in the commingling product sphere.

Have you ever searched for a product on Amazon and received something that looked nothing like the photo and had none of the specifications that were advertised on its page? The product you receive is likely from another company trying to stiff you by riding the coattails of a more successful product.

Shoppers are taken in by the previous reviews of high-quality materials, and suddenly a flood of negative reviews may shut your shop down.

When participating in Amazon FBA commingling, you must be willing to take the risk that your high-quality products may not be the same as others. Even though the people reviewed your product and gave it a high rating, just as many, if not more, may try to make a quick buck. Always do your research when commingling, and provide an addendum to your product to ensure your customers receive the best quality and prices possible.

Conclusion

As with any company, there are pros and cons to setting up shop with Amazon FBA. Different products have different markets, which means that none of the same advantages and disadvantages apply to the same people. Always research your product and its sales on Amazon before deciding which product to supply.

Much of what Amazon FBA has to offer is automated, which means that you do not have to worry about the work done after the product is sent. Perhaps one of Amazon's greatest features is its customer service. Instead of spending time and money on shipping and customer satisfaction, you can focus on the most important part of your shop: the products.

Along with Amazon's Prime features that are included when you join Amazon FBA, you can also take advantage of its discounts on shipping. Not only do customers receive free shipping to their homes, but sellers can also take advantage of the lower costs.

Because of Amazon's quick delivery, it can handle a potentially unlimited stock to add to its collection. As products come and go into warehouses, you can stack more of your products into the shelves. Amazon's background of amazing service keeps people buying from its site, which creates a larger potential for your shop's growth.

Amazon's FBA program, however, also has several drawbacks that lead back to one thing: money. The fees and costs associated with Amazon FBA are, in our opinion, worth it, but it is wise to keep an eye on how much money you spend just keeping up your shop. Initial fees to send in products and monthly subscriptions to Amazon's great benefits may seem like the best deal you have ever received, but the charges add up, especially when sellers continuously add to their shops without receiving a correspondingly high number of sales.

Amazon's free return policy attracts many who want to try out a product with no fear of impending fees, but this often results in return fees that also build up regularly. Since it is more difficult to track inventory with Amazon, you may not be aware of which marketing strategy is failing and resulting in poor reviews. It becomes more difficult to keep everything in order when your business takes off, so constantly perform research.

The sales tax that differs with each state can be complicated and often requires a professional to sort out. The different warehouses that hold your products may change inventory at any time, also preventing easy tax information.

To make packaging easier, many choose to commingle their products with other sellers. However, if you are not careful, other sellers may create accounts that diminish the quality of your product, kicking the product out of

Amazon altogether. In the end, research into your chosen field and Amazon market can help prevent this.

Chapter 5: Creating a Seller Account on Amazon

Now that you have decided on a career with Amazon FBA, the next step is to get everything set up. Amazon's easy-to-use platform makes it easy to create accounts, and setting up the rest of the information is a breeze. This guide will help you to create the best account for you before selling your first product.

Getting Started

Amazon provides several ways to create a seller account that all lead to the same link: services.amazon.com. Follow one of these three ways to complete registration.

1. Navigate to services.amazon.com. Once there, select Start Selling and complete the signup process.

2. Navigate to sellercentral.amazon.com. Click on the blue Register Now button, which will take you to the services.amazon.com link. Select Start Selling to sign up.

3. Navigate to Amazon's homepage, amazon.com. Scroll down to the bottom of the page and find the section listed Make Money with Us. From there, select Sell on Amazon, which will send you to services.amazon.com. Select Start Selling to set up an account.

Individual and Professional Seller Accounts

The next step is to register as either an individual or a professional seller. Either way, you will receive payment from Amazon when selling goods, but the fees associated with subscriptions and listings are slightly different. So how do you decide which seller account is right for you?

A professional seller account is for business people who are in it for the long haul. If you plan to spend the majority of your time with Amazon and reap the benefits of a fully-functional business through one of the greatest online shops of all time, a professional account is right for you. A professional account only costs $39.99 for subscription fees each month, which means that if you are interested in selling many products through Amazon, the subscription is just a drop in the bucket compared to the money you can make selling products. Professional sellers are people who have experience selling and have sold more than a few products with shops of their own or have experience in the field. If you are not sure about whether you will need a professional seller account, hold off for a few months and give an individual account a try before fully committing.

An individual account with Amazon FBA will give you the freedom of selling with Amazon without the monthly subscription. With an individual account, you do not need to pay a monthly subscription. Instead, you are charged $1.00 for every product you sell. You receive all the same services that a professional would receive, but you are not locked into a monthly subscription. Most individual seller accounts are held by people who are only selling one product at a time or are just starting in the business realm. Selling smaller numbers of products eventually justifies the use of an individual seller account. However, if you start to sell more than you first thought, consider switching to a professional account. One dollar per sold product eventually adds up, and it is wiser to set up a professional account if you sell more than 40 products each month.

There are many other differences between individual and professional accounts, so how will you know which one is right for you? Consider the following differences to decide which account to start.

Shipping Rates: It only makes sense that those who have fully subscribed can access the best shipping rates from Amazon. Consider the last time you sold something on Amazon. If you were only interested in selling one thing, the item listed may have come with a standard shipping fee, which is usually $3.99 for standard shipping. Professional sellers with Amazon FBA are lumped into Prime's free two-day shipping, which gives them exclusive discounted shipping rates. If you send packages to Amazon frequently, you may consider moving to a professional account.

Listing New Products: Along the same lines as commingling, individual sellers only have the option of listing their own products with those that have been listed before. If you have recently set up a new shop with curly toe rings that have never been seen before, you must open a professional account. If you are new to the Amazon FBA selling game, you may find it beneficial to start with already-created products to jumpstart your career.

Gated Categories: The so-called gated categories available on Amazon are only available to professional sellers. These categories include "Automotive & Powersports, Collectible Books, Collectible Coins, Entertainment Collectibles, Fine Art, Gift Cards, Jewelry, Music & DVD, Major Appliances, Sports Collectibles, Streaming Media Players, Video, DVD, & Blu-ray, and Watches" (BuyBox, 2019). Though the list may seem small, it includes a vast majority of common items. To sell products in these categories, switch to a professional account.

Streamline Registration

Luckily, registration for a seller account with Amazon FBA is easy and can be completed quickly. However, there is some information necessary to complete the account, and it is best to have it on hand.

Personal Information: Just as with any registration these days, you are required to include personal information from which Amazon can recognize your account. This includes your name, phone number, mailing address, and email address. The information supplied helps Amazon determine which fees, costs, and payments are directed to your account.

Personal Bank Card: This could include a debit or credit card. Amazon's subscriptions and fees are processed as soon as the information is listed in your account and you have set up your first products. You must include a valid billing address and expiration date or Amazon will cancel the registration.

Tax Information: Amazon requires a tax identification number, which is usually associated with a social security number. Amazon must send a tax form to the United States IRS to provide evidence that you are selling products on their platform. Though they walk you through a 1099-K tax form, they are not responsible for withholding taxes for you. Once you start selling with Amazon FBA, it is your responsibility to send in tax information on the state and federal levels.

Setting Up Your Profile

Once completed, you can access your account at any time through the seller portal at sellercentral.amazon.com. You can change any information you would like, and you can adjust the settings to make your shop more accessible to you and your customers. Though it is not necessary to change any settings within the Amazon FBA portal, spend some time perusing its contents. There are likely some areas that require adjusting.

Account Info

All of your seller information is listed in the Account Info section of your seller account. If you need to change your name, mailing address, phone number, or email address at any time, do so here. The Edit button listed on the right side of your account information changes your information as requested.

One of the most important components of the Account Info settings is the Return Information subcategory. Do not become sucked into the fantasy that all customers will want to keep your products without exception. If Amazon is your chosen destination for returns, make sure it is specified in your account info. If you have not set up return shipping preferences, you may see a lot of products ending up on your door.

Make sure that your credit card information is correct on your seller account, or you may not sell on Amazon. Credit cards are set to expire, so inevitably, your credit card will change. If this does happen, change the information in your Account Info section. Keep in mind that Amazon may suspend your account for up to 24 hours if you do not notify them first. They will be able to anticipate the change in card number, and you may not experience the suspension.

Notification Preferences

It is a universal truth that once you sign up for anything, you are sure to be flooded with emails. Amazon is no exception. With constant changes in policy and updated terms of service, you may see an Amazon email more often than you would like. To change this, use the Notification Preferences button to change how many emails you receive from Amazon. You can specify what emails should be sent to you, and you may limit the number of emails to a manageable amount.

Remember that emails that come from Amazon are not frivolous. Those changes in policies or terms of service may negatively affect you, and you may see a deviation from normal practices. For instance, in March 2019, Amazon made an addendum to its previous storage policy. They offered a limited-time opportunity for sellers to test out new products and they would not be charged the additional storage fees. However, this limited-time offer was only available for select items and for only those who took notice. If you miss an opportunity such as this, you may find yourself paying far more than you realize.

Amazon also keeps a record of movement in your shop. This means if someone tries to contact you or there is an overwhelming issue with your products, you will be notified. However, if you do not have the proper notifications set up, you may never receive important emails. Though Amazon does keep track of everything that occurs within your store, you are responsible for keeping it up to date with improved products and better response times.

Gift Options

Amazon allows you to create gift options for your products. To sellers who provide products from their own homes, the option allows sellers to send personalized messages. However, you may need the assistance of a professional to help you set up this feature.

Shipping Settings

Amazon FBA sellers with professional accounts are free to set their own prices for shipping if they are not involved with Amazon Prime shipping. It is possible to make a tidy profit from charging high prices for shipping, and many use this approach. However, take heed of what customers will allow. For example, if you charge $60 for a product that commingled with other sellers, it is less likely that you will sell your product.

Customers are often convinced that free shipping will help their overall savings. While this is not the case, it does provide an opportunity to charge customers extra on the product with the illusion that they are paying less overall.

Tax Settings

To maintain a legal organization, remember correct tax settings are one of the fundamental pillars of a successful business. Why? If you take care of it right away, you will not suffer penalties or become confused with the changing laws. If you start with an alternative tax calculator at the start of your FBA experience, you will not need to worry about changing them later, potentially saving you days of work.

The state in which you need to apply tax information is up to your accountant to decide. At the very least, you need to pay state taxes for your residential state. Other states may claim the right to your taxes if you qualify under their sales tax nexus. A sales tax nexus is essentially a legal term for taxation of products or uses within a location. Think of it as the state charging you for using their roads and property. For example, if you live in New Mexico and use the storage facility in Arizona, Arizona may claim state tax nexus in association with your business.

Be aware that a sales tax nexus is connected to Amazon FBA because inventory storage and drop shipping apply to all Amazon warehouses. Since warehouses are located all over the United States, it is especially important to consider how much tax money has to be set aside in each state. Utilize the services of an accountant to set up the proper tax settings. Tax information can become difficult to track, so an accountant is the safest bet when entering your tax preferences.

User Permissions

As an Amazon FBA professional, you may require employees to have access to some information regarding your account. As soon as you start hiring employees, you can add them as users to your account. Employees have their own login credentials and are only able to see exactly what you want them to see. This means that you decide how involved they are in your corporation.

Amazon has created a list of permissions that other employees are able to view, which range from unlimited to extremely limited. For example, if your partner wants access to your shared account, you can give him or her full access. An employee just responsible for sorting inventory may not have the same permissions but can still have access to the company site.

Be careful who you allow to access your account. If you decide to fire an employee, you must immediately discontinue their account on Amazon or they may gain access to your business.

Info and Policies

Once you start your online store, it is common to enter information about yourself. Though not altogether necessary, it does encourage customers to come back to you if they know a little more about your company. Use the About section to explain who you are, where your company started, and the qualities that set you apart from other sellers, which may include where your products are from and how you describe your style. Many customers like to know about the company from which they are buying, so take some time to hash out these details.

The policies listed on your webpage may include warranty or terms of use, though the area is wide open for any type of policy you wish to use. All Amazon products also contain an FAQ section, which provides an excellent opportunity for you to answer typical questions. Many sellers forgo writing policies because customers will typically ask those questions later, even if the policy is expressly given.

Feedback

Once you have reviewed all settings, you can begin to sell on Amazon. People from all over the world may order your products, and the reviews will start flooding in. Customers tend to base their purchases on the reviews from others, which means that one bad review— particularly in the early selling stages—could sour others to your products.

Amazon offers a way to calculate feedback, but it is far more useful to use a free outside source to find out what people think of your products. Sites such as SellerLabs, FeedbackFive, and FeedbackExpress are all excellent to start learning about your reviews. Be a step ahead of the game by having a marketing strategy based on feedback from your customers.

Conclusion

Getting started with Amazon FBA may seem like a lot to handle, but planning out which path you want to take before you even begin can prevent loss of time and energy. If you are just starting out and are unsure of what products you want to sell, begin with an individual account and base your decisions on the feedback you receive from Amazon and customers. If you already have an established business, consider choosing the professional account. Not only will it save you money on large orders, but you can all set preferences for shipping and new products. If you are serious about becoming a full-time Amazon FBA seller, consider the perks of establishing a professional account.

Though it is unnecessary to set up all the information in your account, your life will become significantly easier if you take the time to read through the options. Basic account changes and notification preferences may seem menial, but they could eventually save you a lot of time and money. Remember that, though you have the option to hide annoying notifications, most are necessary to becoming fully aware of changes and products.

Set your gift options and shipping and tax settings early to prevent future frustration. Much of Amazon is handled by the professionals, but correct tax and shipping settings may prevent inconveniences and lawful action. If you do not check for anything else, update your tax information and verify it with an accountant. You may be saving yourself from days or weeks of work by checking it before you start to sell.

As employees become more necessary with the growth of your shop, set up user information and grant them access to only necessary information. You can change the settings at any time, and disabling past employees' accounts is vitally important to keep a working account. While you are there, leave information about yourself and your policies so customers can learn to trust in the products you give them.

Always monitor the feedback you receive from customers. As we have mentioned before, marketing is one of the most important aspects of your selling account with Amazon FBA. If people do not know about your products, they will not purchase them. Keeping up with feedback can give you a leg up, allowing you to visualize what customers want to see.

Chapter 6: Product Research

The best way to get your business up and running is through finding and selling a profitable product. If you are working to do market research on your own, you will know that it is easier said than done. Finding the perfect product that will stun customers and provide the road to financial freedom is exceedingly difficult if you do not have the right tools, and most people do not.

So how do you find that magical product that will earn you that golden ticket? Market research is essential for distributing a product that people love. Think about an item you have been coveting or merchandise that you see others falling over. That is the beginning of product research: observation. Now, those keen powers of observation become wildly more valuable when you apply them to internet marketing.

Market Research

When it comes to finding the right product, there is only one rule: There is no right product. Many people spend far too much time trying to track down a product that is going to solve their financial burdens without realizing that there is no such product. It all depends on what is trending and how you market the product.

If you are new to market research, it may seem overwhelming to put in hours, if not days, of work to find out which products are trending. However, if you take your time to not only find products but also observe how others market products, you will be surprised about how much you learn.

Define Your Audience

You would not market a hunting knife to a vegan, and you certainly would not market giraffes to crocodile enthusiasts. To market efficiently, you need to understand your audience. Most people make the mistake of generalizing their products and simply marketing them to the community at large. However, if you want to see changes in your selling averages, narrow down your audience using the following audience types.

- Gender
- Age
- Location
- Pay Range
- Family Size
- Career Description
- Activity Levels

These are but a few of many descriptors that you can use to analyze the market you are trying to reach. Pick a group with which you relate. When customers see that you are willing to relate with them in the marketing scheme, they will be more likely to purchase your product.

If you are just starting out, use a spreadsheet to separate the characteristics of your audience, using at least 30 descriptors. Since there are many millions of people who shop at Amazon every year, you have to be specific about your marketing choice. Even if you narrow down the marketing funnel to people who have had smallpox and have ridden in an ambulance, you are sure to meet some expectations. Many marketers err on the side of caution and provide too general an approach to attract specific people.

Survey Your Audience

If you are just starting a business, use social media to interact with friends and acquaintances and use paid advertising to garner a following. Once you have a significant number of people to start a survey group, ask your audience what new or old devices they would like to see. Note the people who have volunteered to answer your survey. Do these people live in different locations, have different habits, or lie in different age groups? Take the information you learn from surveys to market a product that will guide you toward the people most interested in your merchandise.

Engage Your Audience

Once you have set up a following, promote your willingness to listen to their ideas. Most people are more likely to become loyal customers if you offer personal support. Provide avenues for easy access to your audience. If you are just starting, use your influence in your community to find out what people look for the most. Offer appreciative feedback when someone is willing to take the time to talk with you.

If you already have a solid backing in sales, you might already have a customer base from which to interview. In this case, offer incentives to encourage them to tell you how you can improve your products. Many advertisements on social media use this strategy to improve their results. Often, they present awards for people who give reviews of their products and thank those who participated.

When improving upon the performance of a single product, reach out to customers who bought it in the past and ask them for a review of your product. If they offer advice that could potentially help you increase sales or enhance the product itself, present them with newer versions of the product at a discounted price or free. Helpful advice, then, has an incentive for both you and the customers.

Prepare Research Questions

When participating in a study, when was the last time you had to answer a 45-question survey with questions such as "Why do you like me?" Chances are that you did not finish the study. There is a reason why surveys are short and sweet. People have always had limited attention spans, but with the constant distractions of today, it is even more difficult to convince someone to participate in a research project.

Prepare your research questions ahead of time and write out as many as you can. Do not worry, not all of them will make the final cut.

In fact, you should use this opportunity to combine like entries to create killer questions that answer more than one question at a time. Each question should be shaped to inspire the participant to think. Simple yes or no answers often tell you very little, and they often have the effect of leading a customer to think one way or another. Ask questions that will not only ask questions about the product but about the person as well. Use the following guidelines for the perfect survey.

Background Information: What can you learn about this person? You are better able to market to your audience when you know a little bit about them, such as the considerations listed above. Their age or location may not seem vastly helpful, but it can guide you to the right people when you market.

Awareness: What problems can you fix? When you are leading up to questions regarding your products, you need to understand the participant's point of view. What problems do they have that you can solve? If you are marketing for an in-home sleep apnea machine, ask about the person's problems with sleeping, their sleeping habits, other medical issues, etc. Each participant's response creates other possible avenues to people who would be interested in your product.

Consideration: What other alternatives and research has your audience explored? Understand your audience by looking into the same websites, books, and markets that participants have suggested. You can find new ways to improve your product and offer features that other products do not.

Decision: How did the customer make it to your market? Customers usually follow a winding line of research before settling on a decision. Whether they have made it to your store or you are simply looking for ways to market to an audience, ask the participants how they made a final decision on the product they purchased.

Identify Competitors

Whether this means stores in your local area or highly-respected internet brands, the only way to drive customers to your site over others is through identifying who is outpacing you in sales. Visit stores and online platforms to find out who these competitors are and how they market to their customers. Make the most of your experience by asking questions and exploring ways to improve upon their performance.

Many websites employ content marketers to help them boost sales. Why? Because their content usually answers questions and the articles contain search engine optimization keywords to drive competitors to their sites. Identify the top content competitors and make changes to your products that will satisfy most audiences. As a bonus, many people leave reviews for content writing at the bottom of the page that you can use to answer questions before they arise.

Profitable Products and Selling Mistakes

Once your market research is complete (or during your market research), it is time to pick a profitable product. Since there is no right answer when selecting a product, find something that you are passionate about and capitalize on the funds. The best way to sell a product is to find one you love and simply explain why you feel so strongly about it.

Common Errors

When selecting a product, most people get hung up on a lot of superfluous problems when finding a product, which makes selling impossible. Consider it this way: If you cannot find a product to sell, you will never be a great Amazon FBA seller. Avoid these common mistakes to get out of that slump.

<u>*Believing the Perfect Product Myth:*</u> If you are a perfectionist, you know what we are talking about. It can seem paralyzing to not settle for the best. However, if you only focus on what product will make the most profit, you will find yourself waiting for a long time. Your job is to find a product that will sell quickly, *any* product. After you have done your market research, you should feel at least somewhat comfortable with your options. Sell the product that hits you in the gut as the product you can market the best.

Information Overload: This book has already given you a lot of tips about what you should know and how to make the best choices with Amazon FBA. However, do not let this lead you into information overload. If you find yourself wondering how the rest of the world figured it out and you did not, it is time to take a break. Do not drown yourself in endless marketing techniques and possibilities. Take a chance with instinct after you have been given the best information possible.

Thinking Too Generally: Suffocating under the assumption that you must choose one category instead of one product often leads to frustration. If your question is whether you should focus on phone cases or fans, you are thinking too generally. Focus first on one product. Once you have found the product you wish to sell, focus on that product until you have mastered its marketing. From there you can start to build your empire.

Following the Herd: When one product explodes on the market, it is only natural to assume that you can make money from that product as well. However, consider the repercussions if everyone thought the same way: There would be an abundance of personalized kitchen washcloths with no homes. Pave your own way and make it unique to your circumstances.

Avoiding Future Forecasting: Future forecasting refers to a seller's ability to project his or her profits. This includes product purchases, fees, monthly costs, and projected products sold. Become aware of your financials before you sell even one product. Many believe that if they offer the lowest price possible, they will have the hottest-selling commodity. While that may be true, it does not mean that they will make a profit from selling the products.

Product Parameters

When selecting a product, be aware of the product's parameters. Remember, you want to find a product that will cost you as little as possible to store but as much as possible to sell. The criteria are ultimately up to you, but here are some suggestions to a more cost-effective product selection.

Start Small: When starting your journey as an Amazon FBA seller, remember that much of your money will go to fees if you do not sell your products quickly. For that reason, start with smaller products. Choose a product that is less than 15 oz to start. Shipping and handling fees will be much smaller for a standard-size package. Though standard shipment is for a package less than two pounds (or 32 oz), stay on the small side to avoid excessive fees.

Charge Reasonably: You might notice that many people who charge less than $10 seem to either sell quite a few products or hardly any, and the reason for that is two-fold: People either jump at the chance of a deal, or they think the product is cheap and therefore not worth their money. When charging customers for products, many people choose to sell products in the $15 - $100 range, which is highly reasonable. But, if you are looking to increase your profits and still provide an incentive for customers to buy your products, try selling products in the $20 - $75 range. The prices are still reasonable, and you make enough money to pay Amazon's fees while still making a profit.

Product Profitability

In order for a product to be profitable, you must sell it at a price higher than what you bought it. Of course, this is a no-brainer. But, when deciding at what price to sell it, consider the 3x rule. You want to sell your products at three times the amount for which you bought it. You want to cover the costs and fees Amazon charges and still come out on top.

Narrow Your Product Research Area

Now that you have mastered the basics of what you should look for, it is time to shop. With a wide realm of products to research and very little time to sell everything you wish, narrow down your product research area.

There are two potential ways to pick a product: finding a product within a niche and advertising through its market group or simply choosing a product and working from there. Both are highly profitable, but we will focus on the former of these two. Look for a product in a group that will allow you to both express your personality and relate to the people who share your interests.

If you are still unsure about what niche best suits you, take a look at Amazon's home page. The advertisements for products show that there is a good bet that those products are doing well enough to support the use of ads. Again, do not get sucked into the notion that everything that is profitable for someone else is going to be profitable for you, but they are a good guideline to show you which products are succeeding.

Avoid the restricted items in Amazon. In Chapter 5, we briefly mentioned the gated categories. Though it is possible to sell items on this list, spend the majority of your time focused on other products. These products often include extra permissions for shipping and selling that make it more difficult to sell in a timely manner.

Select the Correct Online Tools

When selling on Amazon, you will not only be using the internet for selling. In fact, use your resources to find the best material possible when selecting products. Plenty of Amazon FBA success stories start with finding a product that is worthy of their time and easy to market. To find more success, use the following tools.

StartupBros Workbook: StartupBros provides an excellent workbook to help you narrow down your search for products. It is completely free and offers advice about how to start up your own business. Their spreadsheet provides training to help you on your way to Amazon FBA success.

JungleScout   Product   Research   Tool: JungleScout offers a paid training session with some of the best tools out there. They offer lessons, classes, and analytic tools, among others. They also offer an extension for your internet to help you find the best products. JungleScout is one of our top sites, so be sure to visit.

Unicorn Smasher Product Research Tool: This free service also helps to analyze sales with different products. One of its best features is its price. It is not as thorough as JungleScout, but it still offers a great extension for Chrome.

Conclusion

Before you even begin buying products, do some research into what the best products might be. Remember, there is no perfect product, so just choose one! To finally start your journey as an Amazon FBA seller, you need to have the products to sell, and you will never find one if you are too picky.

The market research you perform should make the most of the world around you. When you are looking for the perfect product, do not stop at browsing through Alibaba. You might find some products that you like, but many stop because they feel overwhelmed by the options. Ask your friends, neighbors, and social media following what they think about products today. Ask what they would like to see, how they would like their world to improve with a new product, or simply find something fun.

When conducting surveys, always pay attention to the questions you ask. Remember, you want to create a survey experience that is short but still gets you the answers you need. Find out each person's background to see how you should market your product, and use paid surveys for incentives if you are feeling ambitious.

When choosing a product, do not fall into common pitfalls such as wasting too much time narrowing down your search. Have some fun with the market research and find new online tools that will help you.

Make a profit on your products by following the 3x rule. Be sure, however, to keep the resulting price reasonable for your customers. They will not want to buy $300 products if they can find cheaper options with the same quality. Your customers depend on finding the best product for the best price, so be sure to beat the competition while still making a tidy profit.

Chapter 7: Niche

With all the products from which to choose, why would you want to sell within a niche? There are thousands of people spread across the globe who are looking for products that you are selling. Whether they are refined to canvas drawings of monkeys or are merely interested in finding a dog suit for the next furry event, everyone has a product that speaks to them.

What Is a Niche?

A niche is a subsection of a larger group. For example, if we were to use the same shirt example, you may choose to use a more descriptive term, such as a peasant blouse. This niche is a subcategory of the larger group, and breaking the term down into more descriptive terms makes it easier for customers to find your product.

There are millions of niches of which to take advantage, and now is the time to get started with your search. Take a concept for a product, such as the shirt, and narrow it down into specific subcategories. The more unique your subcategory is, the less likely that someone will have already developed a product for it.

Tips to Find a Niche

Since niches are so important to creating leads, it is important to spend as much time as you need to find the perfect one. Finding a niche is not an easy task, and more often than not, you will see the results for searched keywords are commonly used by other companies. However, this is the perfect opportunity to see what other competitors are saying and how you can become a cut above the rest.

Find your groove in a niche that is specific to your tastes by following products you are passionate about. You can become an advocate for your product while building your brand. Though finding a niche may be difficult, it is well worth the time. Below are tips to find your niche.

Seasonality Slumps

When searching for a niche, be aware that there are many seasonal products that will ultimately hurt your sales numbers. Consider, for example, selling a snowman decoration in the middle of July. The chances are that either you will sell none, or you will hit the jackpot with someone who is really excited about the Christmas season. On the other hand, if you sell a hot product such as exercise leggings, you will likely see much steadier results throughout the year.

When selecting a niche, select products that show the best results. You can easily find these results with a simple Google search if you know what to look for. Thousands, if not millions, of sites provide information on the best-selling products of the year, month, or week. However, remember not to pick only one website in which to do your research. The more information you glean from various websites, the more likely you are to find accurate projections.

Profit Margins

We all know that selling the most profitable item will bring in the big bucks. But how do you negotiate what your cost will be versus how much to sell? The 3x rule is an excellent start, but we will dive deeper.

Consider selling a pen on Amazon for $2.00 when it only cost you $0.05. Surely you are getting the best deal possible for the sale! However, consider the amount of money it takes to ship and keep the pens stored at Amazon. Though this might seem like a good deal, always remember to analyze how much profit you make after fees and costs. As a general rule, anything above a 15% profit margin is considered good.

Competing Videos

One of the best marketing tools is advertising videos on YouTube and social media. Why? People are more likely to watch a video than read a long post. Grabbing an audience with exciting videos makes potential customers more likely to buy.

However, there is a catch: Competing companies will be using the same strategy. To set yourself apart from the rest of the crowd, you must find a niche in which to sell your products. Large categories and general subjects deflect from your products and often create such a long list that potential customers have to wade through several hundred videos to find yours. This becomes exceptionally harder when they have the views that you do not.

Marketing a product in a niche is important to your overall sales because it narrows down your search parameters to bring customers to your product. Consider marketing for vanilla candles. When plugged into a Google search, the results yield nearly 500,000 results that range from making them yourself to advertisements for large companies. What does that mean for you? It means that you will have to create the largest ad campaign to beat out the already-established companies that thought of marketing for vanilla candles in the first place. Narrowing your search to vanilla cake candle cuts the number of Google video results by nearly half.

Be specific about the keywords that you use as well. Find words that most of your competitors are less likely to choose. For example, imagine you want to sell products related to your favorite monster (we are going to assume that is the manticore). When shoppers search for "monster products," they receive over 17 million results, but when they search for "manticore products," the video results reduce to around 13,000. Use your imagination when looking into your product niche.

Product Dimensions

As noted previously, the dimensions of your products are extremely important to consider. You must find a product that will be profitable but will also not weigh much. The niche you decide should properly reflect small dimensions.

If you are looking to enter the carpentry sales category, consider how much your product will set you back if you expect to sell only 3-meter bookshelves. First of all, you will have to pay for the oversized storage. Next, consider how likely it is that someone will buy your product. You may have spent over $500 bringing your bookshelf overseas, and it may take six months or more to sell the product. What is more, you will have to charge at least $1,500 to follow the 3x rule and pay for all storage and shipping fees.

Customers are no more likely to want to lug a large object around the house than you are to sell it. Most of the time, customers opt for smaller products on online sites. They are cheaper, and they are faster to ship. Also, smaller objects are less likely to be damaged (if they are naturally sturdy like our bookshelf example).

Sponsored Products

One of the most satisfying parts of research is finding a successful product that has an abundance of helpful keywords. Search engine optimization (SEO) is the leading cause of finding products. For example, if you are looking for a weighted blanket on a search engine like Google, you will find products that match your keyword on the first page. People all over the United States are hired to complete a simple task: Make a website more easily found in a search engine.

Because of SEO, creating a way to find your product is more difficult than ever. SEO provides a way for competitors to market their products, and if you are just starting out, you may find it difficult to market a product that uses many of the same keywords as others. For instance, defining your product by the keyword "shirt" may describe your product the best, but there are guaranteed to be millions of other entries for the same keyword. And that is where a niche comes in handy.

When marketing your product, use unique keywords to express your product effectively, and bring people to your product by giving them other options. Your niche becomes your corner of the market to which customers can come and make unique purchases.

It should be a no-brainer that you want to find a product that is in demand, otherwise, no one will think to find it. For example, one of the biggest products of 2019 was leggings. If you look at Amazon's products, you'll notice that there are thousands of results for leggings, but only one stands out. Why? It is because the company listened to customers and offered them leggings that were reasonably priced and with the right material. Though leggings were a hot item, one company thrived more than the rest and created a demand for these leggings.

That brings us to another point: If there is no demand for a product, find a way to make it more desirable. Common household tools are often replaced because of breakage or cheapness. If you decide to make your living by selling spatulas, make them stand out among the others. Common examples may include turning everyday items into animals or creating indestructible products. What was the last time you ditched one of your tools for something cuter or of better quality?

Niche Idea Search

One of the most fun parts of creating or joining a niche is searching for products that fit within your scope. It is common to feel as though you have no idea what you want to choose, so do not become discouraged. Find that one product you have faith in and become its advocate. Follow these steps that will help you define your niche.

Identify Your Passions: We have rehashed this many times in this book because it is one of the most important ways that you can develop your store. Find at least ten products that you like and write them down in a list, writing down their pros and cons. Remember, you are trying to narrow down your search, so do not write down more than 30 ideas with the hopes that you will find one that suits your personality better.

Business is difficult, and starting from scratch can be extremely frustrating. Choosing a product for which you have no passion makes it that much harder to keep your head up. Think about what products you have seen in the media, on magazine covers, or down the street at your cousin Fred's house. Gain inspiration from people around you to narrow your search even more.

Identify Solvable Problems: Think like an inventor. Look at your everyday life and see what products you could create or distribute that would make someone else's life easier. What problems can you solve with the products you sell?

If you find yourself wondering if you can overcome some of the problems that arise from the malfunctioning product, it is a safe bet to pass on it. Problems arise in all merchandise, so selling a product you do not know how to use may result in more problems than it solves. For example, cheap technology does not often perform well after extensive use. You could sell the products just as they are, but you may see a lot of bad reviews and lower ratings. Stand firm behind a product to present the best quality you can.

Interview people around you and in online forums to see what problems the average person experiences in a day. Take note of the ages, locations, and statuses of all participants to get the most out of each survey. Note how you can make their lives better by providing them with a product that is affordable and worth the money.

Niche Profitability: After you have narrowed your search down to the final few results, look at the profitability of each niche. If you see pot holders selling for $5.00 each, it is a good bet that you will not make much money on the product, assuming you provide the same quality as everyone else. Become confident in your niche by seeing how profits rise and fall throughout the year. Use Google to analyze stocks for similar products to see if the companies are seeing increases or decreases for selling those items.

Test on Amazon: When you have finished your list, take some of them for a test drive. This means only sending some to Amazon. If you find that you gain profits from your chosen product, continue to send it in. Choosing the right niche may take several tries, but keep at it until you are successful.

Conclusion

When finding the right product for your Amazon FBA store, consider starting with a niche. You will find that you are better able to market to your selected audience when you know who your audience is. Market research becomes much easier when you narrow your results down to only a few options that fit your market.

When finding a niche that works for you, take your time to carefully study websites and Amazon itself to find products that are the most successful. Usually, the right product and atmosphere are right under your nose.

Consider what your niche can do for you. For example, if you want a big payout for a product that you adore, you need to keep in mind how marketable your passion product really is.

Understand that the products you choose are there to work for you, not the other way around. Do not get hung up on which niche is the most profitable if you do not recognize which product is the most profitable. Remember, you are selling products, not niches. Use your niche to market your products and use advertisements for the right people, but do not expand your operation before you know which product to sell.

Chapter 8: Suppliers

Suppliers will become some of your best friends as you continue within the realm of Amazon FBA. You cannot sell products that you do not have. So how close are you with your suppliers? With the tools you have learned in previous chapters, you are now ready to negotiate with potential suppliers.

Now that you have narrowed down which products you want to sell, the next step is to find the products you need. You can create your own or have them shipped to you, at which point you resell them. Since it is wise to look for inexpensive materials and products, many people order products from overseas. Wholesale sites are also common, but they often require buying in bulk to get a good price on products.

Wholesales

Creating a product base by wholesaling is highly effective, and it may promise some of the greatest rewards. If you are new to selling, however, it is probably best to wait until you have a decent following before you start selling wholesale products. That said, if you have a firm background in marketing and know how to sell yourself, this may be the best option for you.

Buying wholesale has four main benefits: Creating a connection with one wholesale company often opens the door for additional company connections, selling wholesale products often has a proven track record on which you can capitalize, you can often buy as many products as you want, and you can sell the same products over and over again.

The Four Benefits

Sell the Same Products: A successful business on Amazon involves finding a product that sells well and sticking to it. Essentially, if you find a wholesaler that is willing to work with you, you have the chance to sell the same products over and over again with similar results throughout the year. Others may consider this to be the holy grail of sales. If you can find a product that satisfies customers and the company with whom you work, you can maintain a fruitful business with Amazon FBA.

The Great Track Record: Unfortunately, many people sell inferior products on Amazon; just look on the internet for failed online shopping. This often results in negative reviews and an unsuccessful business on the Amazon platform. However, with wholesales, you already know the quality of the product from past reviews and sales information. With a well-established brand, you are more likely to see sales. Shoppers like to stick with what they know, and if they have used that brand for years, they are likely to use it again and again.

For example, consider a trusted brand such as KitchenAid. They have had consistently high sales over the years, and their products have changed very little. They maintain a stellar track record and are among the top kitchen appliances throughout the world. Buying KitchenAid products wholesale and proving yourself an excellent marketer could mean that you would not have to sell any other brand.

Buy and Buy Again: It is often suggested that you have at least $500 in capital before starting a connection with wholesalers, though more is always better. Companies who wholesale products often require buyers to purchase a large stock. The good news is that once you have sold all of your products, you can always buy more.

Wholesalers keep their sellers interested through major discounts. Usually, you want to find a wholesale product that is 50% of the retail price, and there are companies out there that might beat those discounts. One of the hardest parts of wholesaling, though admittedly the most rewarding, is finding the companies that offer the best prices. Do your research to make the most of wholesale deals. Once you find your perfect company, stick with it.

Creating Connections: Often, companies that believe that you are a good selling partner will also refer you to a sister or like companies. This creates an avenue for you to expand your business over time. If you are successful at selling one product, your reputation will grow, and you will be more in demand from other companies. Companies look for people who have a proven track record, and selling for high-profile companies can land you those coveted roles as a wholesaler for notable brands.

How to Make It

With all of these benefits, it seems insane to try any other method of acquiring products to sell on Amazon, but searching the classifieds for wholesalers is more difficult than it might appear. Wholesalers are often looking for someone that can benefit their company. After all, they do not want to trust someone who will not get the job done, and understandably so. How, then, do you connect with wholesalers to convince them you are the right candidate for the job?

Step 1 - Choose the Company: If you are reselling merchandise, your product is the brainchild of a mother company. Though there may be many sources for the product you want to sell on Amazon, find its originating company. Often, the businesses you want to contact are struggling with one thing or another. There are several ways you can decipher what company you need to contact.

- Amazon ranking is higher than 100
- The product is not found on Amazon
- Products are sold by a third-party seller
- The company is struggling financially

Any of these options could mean that the merchandiser needs help selling their products, which is where you come in.

Step 2 - Communication: Companies that need help will likely welcome a call from a marketer. When selling yourself as a marketer for another company, always make a positive first impression, and that might mean that you need to get out of your comfort zone. The more contact you are willing to make with a company, the more impressed they will become.

If possible, schedule a visit to their company or find a time to talk with a representative. Face-to-face contact is highly desirable, and it is a nice break from the constant stream of emails most companies receive every day. The next best way to communicate is by phone call. Though not quite as personal as face-to-face contact, you are likely to be a step above the rest of the applicants due to that extra personal touch. Finally, if all else fails, send them an email. It is the least personal of the three types of communication, but it still shows some personal touch.

Step 3 - Prove It: You may have heard this many times on the childhood playground, but now is the time to take action. The first step to finding wholesalers to take you in as a seller for their company is to have the right background. Established sellers are more likely to get connections with wholesalers because they have experience growing companies, but that does not mean you cannot do it if you have no experience. Show the company what you can do by writing down marketing techniques and plans to increase their profit. Companies are always looking to improve their sales, so show them you can.

Overseas Private Label Suppliers

Another common way to get supplies is through overseas shipping. It is not surprising that Alibaba is one of the major contributors to these overseas products. Their supplies are cheap, and they ship at a remarkably reasonable rate.

Though Alibaba is one of the most popular overseas companies for retrieving supplies, they are also risky. The quality of the products ranges from well-made to complete disaster. Be careful about what you order through these sites as terrible reviews can prevent you from reaping the rewards of a cheap alternative. However, using materials from these sites to create better alternatives is an excellent way to capitalize on a good deal.

Open an Alibaba Account

As mentioned previously, Alibaba is a common site to purchase affordable materials and products. The first step to ordering from Alibaba is to set up an account. Follow these instructions to get started.

1. Navigate to Alibaba, select menu, and click Join Free.
2. Enter a valid email address and verify your account.
3. Fill out the basic information such as your name, address, phone number, and company name (the company name can be whatever you choose) and select Confirm.
4. Select a payment method from the choices of Trade Assurance, Gold Supplier, and Assessed Supplier (all are secure).

Make sure that you verify with your bank that all information is correct and that you have found the correct supplier for your chosen products.

Your suppliers are the bread and butter of your company, which means that you need to create a line of communication with them to get the best deals possible and to set up a trusted partnership. Though this might scare potential sellers off, communication with suppliers is absolutely essential to good business. When you communicate with suppliers, they are more likely to give you discounts and provide a good foundation from which you can build.

Send an email to your suppliers to get the ball rolling. If you are unsure about what your email should hold, use the following form letter as a basis for your communication.

SUBJECT: Supplier Business Prospect

Dear [NAME(S) HERE]

Though I cannot directly divulge company information such as monthly revenue and supply, my company would like to begin a supplier relationship with yours. From what I have seen of your company, I value the supply you give to other companies, and I would like to open communication with your company.

As a merchant, my company is looking to retrieve 100 - 500 units of [PRODUCT] on a trial basis. Should my company find the product acceptable and wish to continue our relationship, we will request 1000 - 5000 units of [PRODUCT].

We appreciate the time you took to respond to this email and ask that you let us know as soon as possible if this arrangement is reasonable to you. I look forward to continued communication between my company and yours.

Sincerely,

[YOUR NAME]

Remember that your suppliers are also business people, so they are looking for a professional relationship. Do not let this form letter scare you away. Adjust the wording as you see fit to work best with your business.

Set up the expectation that you are the negotiating manager first to set a precedent for future communication. Expressing this kind of authority makes sure that your message goes to the right person.

With your communication lines open, continue to negotiate with your supplier to find the best deals possible. Remember that you always want a sample of the products you are going to receive. These could be anywhere from 5 to 20 products at a time. Shipping for so few items will likely cost you, so expect to receive a shipping fee of $100 - $200. Of course, the higher priority the shipment is, the more money you will have to pay, so do not be surprised if you receive orders in the high hundreds.

Product Launch

When you receive products from both wholesalers and companies overseas, always remember to inspect your products. You do not want to send inferior products to Amazon as part of your first launch. There is a high possibility that at least some of the merchandise is damaged from shipping, so be prepared to either fix products or forsake them altogether.

Conclusion

If you want to become a successful Amazon FBA seller, you have to know where to get useful supplies at a good price. Using wholesale sites or overseas companies are both common ways to acquire supplies for your Amazon FBA business, but you must first know how to negotiate your way through good deals.

First, find a company that best suits your needs. This company must have both the supplies you need and discounts that make the purchases worth it. Companies are easily researched through Amazon and Alibaba, the two titans in the product supply arena. Make sure that you scout out more than one company to find the best deals.

Second, build a basis of communication with each company and establish yourself as a priority seller. Make yourself highly marketable by starting communication with high-ranking officials, and set yourself apart by knowing your product and business. After all the research you have done, you should know your way around your product, so use that knowledge.

Third, take care of your supplies. Though getting your supplies may seem like the hard part, remember that it is your responsibility to make sure that each product is Amazon ready. Alibaba may have some of the best deals on merchandise on the internet; however, the money you save with supplies is often outweighed by the time it takes to ship from China. Keep in mind that your customers come first, so always give them the best.

Chapter 9: How to Sell on Amazon

With all the information you received, you are no doubt ready to begin selling and taking that first step to your future business. Be prepared to shell out some more money when you are starting your business. There are certain package requirements required to sell products on Amazon.

Create an Amazon Listing

We walked through how to set up your Amazon account in Chapter 5, so you are well on your way to your first sale. The next step is to create a listing through Amazon. Work through the following steps to create the perfect listing for your brand.

Step 1 - Amazon's Seller Central: By the end of this book, you should be well acquainted with Amazon's seller central since it is the first place to start your listings. Navigate to sellercentral.amazon.com and select the inventory dropdown menu. The fourth item listed is Add a Product; select it.

Step 2 - Create the Product Listing: You have two options when entering a product: You can either choose a product from the search bar Amazon provides, or you can select to create a new product listing. When setting up your first product, select the create a new product listing option.

Step 3 - Choose a Category: Amazon provides a list of categories that describe products sold on Amazon. Take time to carefully go through this list to find the option that works best for your product. Though it is possible to list a gated item, it is far more tedious than simply choosing a product that will be uploaded immediately. Remember that gated items usually take up to 24 hours to approve.

Step 4 - Fill Out the Required Information: Generally, the required information for products includes the title, manufacturer, brand, and price. Do not feel as though you are required to have all the information right away. All information can be changed since you are not setting up a live account. You are just getting the information listed before sending products to Amazon.

Both the manufacturer and brand names listed can be the name of your company. If you are unsure about what that will be, just write something down. Again, you can change the information later. However, now may be the time to think about the name of your business.

The price listed is entirely up to you. However, make sure to look at the prices listed for similar items on Amazon. You want your price to be as close to the Amazon Prime price as possible, though producing a price that is lower is always the better option. Remember that you can change the price at any time as well.

Step 5 - Buy a UPC Code: A UPC code is the barcode you see on every product for sale in the United States. To become a businessman or woman, you must use UPC codes to mark the products you sell on Amazon. Unique 12-digit UPC codes are available on the internet, but be sure you are using the right website to get the best prices possible. BarcodesTalk and SnapUPC are two common sites that offer UPC codes at reasonable prices. Remember that when you buy in bulk, you receive a bigger discount. However, take your chances with a small amount before purchasing 15,000. Get your feet wet before diving in headfirst.

Step 6 - Product ID: With the newly-purchased UPC code, open the JPEG attached to the number and write the information down in the Product ID section. You can select what type of code the product ID uses, but the standard should be listed as UPC. Once done, select Save and Finish to complete your listing.

Create an FBA Shipping Plan

Once you have set up the majority of your product information with Amazon, you will notice the need to set up a shipping plan. Amazon FBA sellers get discounts with popular shipping companies when they sign up for a professional account, so now is the time to take advantage of those discounts. Use the following directions to set up your shipping plan.

Step 1 - Change to Fulfilled By Amazon: Within the Inventory dropdown menu, select the edit button and check the box listed Change to Fulfilled By Amazon.

Step 2 - Convert Only: A new page will appear after you have switched to Fulfilled By Amazon. In the top right corner, a button will appear that reads Convert Only. Select this button then refresh the page. Once the page finishes loading, check the Inventory dropdown menu again and select Print Item Labels.

Step 3 - Send and Replenish: The packages you send to Amazon may be individually packaged or sent in a large box; it is completely up to you. However, you will most likely save money on shipping if you ship all of your items together. To do this, in your Fulfilled By Amazon menu, select Send and Replenish. Then fill out the ship from supplier field. You can send all products directly to Amazon from your supplier, but it is often better to have the items sent from you. After all, you need to inspect your merchandise before you send it to Amazon.

Step 4 - Shipping Information: You may be required to fill out a Hazmat Review Form which determines what hazardous material is in your shipment. Unless you are dealing with highly toxic or otherwise dangerous material, you should not need to select anything other than NO in the fields requesting the type of hazardous materials sent. Though this form is not always necessary, it is wise to fill out the form just in case. Since it is likely your product is not hazardous, the form should not take long to fill out.

Find the dimensions of your shipping boxes. You are not required to know the specifications down to the millimeter, so give a rough estimate of each size. Do not, however, provide wild guesses. The space given for the dimensions of your products is measured in inches, so provide information that is somewhat accurate down to the inch. Also include the number of items in your box.

Next, Amazon will request information regarding prep. They essentially want to know if Amazon will need to do any of the prep work. Since you should be inspecting all of your products, the answer should be NO. Do not rack up extra fees by making Amazon do your prep for you. All the labels should be completed by the manufacturer, which is you. When filling out this section, make sure to mention that you will be doing all of the work.

Step 5 - Shipment Options: When asked how you will ship the items, fill out the company you will use to ship your products. The most common choice is UPS for its speed and reliability, but USPS often offers cheaper options, so choose wisely.

Amazon Product Photography

Photographs are required when listing a product, so be sure to have all the photographs you need before you start the listing. Create the best product by giving customers the best information about your product through images. One of the most important parts of a product is its photography. Think about the last product you bought online. Would you have bought it if there had not been a photograph attached to it? Customers often believe photos are the make-or-break factors of a product. For example, many search for vehicles online, but few even click on ads for vehicles with less than five photos.

Shoppers want to see what they are buying, and that goes for any product online. The best bet you have for selling a product is to provide the customer with as much detail as you can. If you have a limited budget for photos, consider reducing the amount, but try to stay above three total photos for each product.

Many companies offer professional photography for all products you wish to sell, and many of them have decent prices for the work. For instance, Product Photography offers services that are as low as $24 per image. Additional product photography sites often offer these kinds of deals, but you will have to shop around to find the prices that are right for you.

Amazon also provides professional product photography for any and all of your merchandise, but it does come at a cost. Five photos are priced at $250, so it does require some financial backing to get the best bang for your buck. However, if you can afford it, professional photography by Amazon may be worth it.

If you feel a tug at your purse strings, you can always take the photos yourself. There are thousands of online videos to help you create your own professional photos. Try to provide photos that show as much detail as possible for the best results. Also, local photographers are likely to give excellent prices for taking photos. Consider giving local businesses a chance with the same excellent results.

Product Listing Optimization

Though you may have the best product on the market and offer the best prices, without product listing optimization, it is unlikely that you will receive as many views as you hope. Fortunately, there are several ways to improve your product listing so you can achieve the best possible results.

Product listing optimization is the process of making your product the highest rated of its kind. Once you have created the listing, just how important is it to create a product that is optimized? The three main reasons to optimize a product are to increase your overall rankings, to bring people to your product, and to ultimately grow sales. So, you could say that product listing optimization is one of the most important parts of listing a product on Amazon. Optimization is a worthy way to spend your time, but we want to create the experience easier for you. Here are some of the key ways to optimize your product listing.

Product Title

When was the last time you purchased a product that had a title like "Goo For Sale"? Though slime has become increasingly popular over the years, that does not mean that you should advertise it as "goo." Think about a name for the title that will inspire people to find what they are looking for.

Chapter 7's discussion of SEO is the perfect introduction to creating a product title that will grab attention. Remember, you want to create a title that is descriptive of your product while maintaining a specific nature. For example, your product title for packaged slime should contain the word "slime" to better direct people to your product, but you can provide greater optimization by adding a descriptor. If your slime has blues and purples with glitter, you may market it as "Galaxy Slime." This will narrow down potential searches and create an attention-grabbing name for potential buyers.

Product Features and Descriptions

As has been discussed multiple times in this book, it is essential to create a listing with a product that has a lot of descriptors. In your description settings, add product dimensions, type of material, styles, and any other descriptors you find necessary. Arrange these into bullet points for easier reading.

Put yourself in the customer's shoes. How will they know that they are buying the right product? If you are unsure of how much information you should add about your product, put your shoes on the customer. What does this mean? Create descriptions with enough detail that your customer can visualize what the product actually feels like. Show customers how much they will love your product by virtually placing them in the same room as your product. Many believe that online shopping will never overtake the experience of physically shopping, so create the moment for them by bringing buyers an unforgettable experience.

Product Results and Ratings

What about your product makes it stand apart from the rest? Many shoppers buy products looking to improve some aspect of their lives. Your product should describe the results that it achieves. Many people are willing to spend a large sum of money for a product that actually works. Encourage reviews to bring people back again and again.

Consider the Indian Healing Clay product on Amazon that has received almost 25,000 ratings with an average star rating of 4.4 out of 5. This simple clay, once mixed with water or apple cider vinegar, is an effective acne reducer. Chances are that you have never seen an ad for this product, but it is still one of the most popular products on the Amazon market. The product has the right balance of cost-effectiveness and positive product reviews that have caused it to make the lists of some of the most popular blogs. They use many descriptors but mostly use the strength of the product to speak for itself.

Create a Brand and Packaging

One of the best ways to sell products is to provide excellent graphics. This applies to both your logo and product designs. Sites like Freeeup and Fiverr are often the best to find talented graphic designers to help you build your brand. Make use of their expertise within a healthy budget for anything you need.

Another way to ensure you make the most out of your product is by creating a packaging design that is unique to you. Many people are impressed by the effort sellers put into small additions. Consider including a thank you note or any other letter within your product to encourage customers to think of you again. In your letter, use your logo or other packaging design to add personality.

Automate Your Amazon FBA Business

Many third-party companies do much of the work for you so you can focus on keeping up your branding through marketing and optimization. This is your business, so automating everything is up to you. You will likely have to shell out money that would otherwise go to your own funds, but other companies save you the trouble of inspecting and shipping products that come in from China and wholesalers.

Third-party companies such as FBA Inspection are commonly used to make your life easier. They offer low prices for each product you would like inspected. Amazon FBA does not allow suppliers to do the inspection for you, so you need to rely on either yourself or a middleman to complete the work. Note that you should only consider this option after you have everything set up in Amazon. You might find yourself paying too much out of pocket to make any profit if you are not comfortably set with your sales.

Conclusion

Before you even sell your products, set up a listing on Amazon. Make sure that the listing is not live before it is published. While setting general information, consider the best way to ship your products to Amazon. Utilize common shipping companies associated with Amazon to get the best discounts and make shipping faster.

When creating listings for Amazon, always remember to use the tools around you to get the most out of your listings. Optimized simple features that Amazon requires on each of its listings could springboard you into a more comfortable market. Taking the time to optimize your listings through selecting unique product titles, relating product features and descriptions effectively, and utilizing Amazon results and ratings will provide a basis for a highly-visited store.

Consider the costs of an effective Amazon shop. If you want to make the most out of every listing, hire the best graphic designers and photographers to make your products pop. Remember, your aim is to create a listing that is pleasing to the eye. High ratings and many reviews are common reasons for page visits, so encourage customers to leave reviews of your products.

Once you have finished setting up your products and have some selling experience under your belt, consider automating your business. You can pay others to inspect your products for you so you can focus on producing the best marketing information possible. Since this is your company, use your best judgment concerning costs to optimize your income while making your life easier.

Chapter 10: Amazon Ads

Whether you work as a marketer or you have been living under a rock, it is almost impossible to miss the ads that pop up on the computer, on billboards, or in any written material. Applications have been made to block ads on your phone or computer because they have become so prevalent in today's society. Why? Because they work.

Customers not only expect to see ads on online shopping sites, but they often respond well to the stimulus. That is because people who enter shopping sites like to see other products for sale. Amazon ads are no exception to the rule. Since it is one of the leading shopping sites in the world, creating ads on Amazon is an excellent way to introduce new customers to your product. And since you are already an Amazon FBA member, you can take advantage of the easy-access advertisements Amazon provides.

What Are Amazon Ads?

Amazon ads are paid, sponsored items that pop up as a result of keyword searches. When you search for an item on Amazon, the platform generates a paid advertisement that coincides with your search. For example, if you wanted to find a purple food that induced long episodes of laughter, you might find advertisements that correspond to "purple," "drink," or "laughter." In this case, the results yielded products related to food coloring and humorous mugs.

Ads are designed to optimize the results of Amazon searches, so be aware of the keywords you use when describing your product. Amazon will use those keywords to make the best possible matches with customer searches.

Are Amazon Ads Worth It?

Consider the last time you spent time on Amazon. Were you swayed by some of the advertisements listed on the home page, or did you make it to the advertisements listed on individual search pages? Either way, it is likely that you have clicked on an ad sometime in your experience with Amazon. So, is it worth it to advertise on Amazon when you have an FBA account? Absolutely! You are already set up with a platform that is designed to help you sell your products, so utilize all the tools that Amazon offers.

Ads generate more clicks for your products, and general studies have noted that interest in your products rises considerably when advertising with paid ads (Whitney, 2019). If you are a first-time seller and do not know where to start with paid advertisements, consult your market research to find trending products. Often, products with these advertisements will also give you a leg up in discovering your own methods for paid advertisements.

Amazon Advert Costs

Like most online advertisements these days, you can set a budget for your ad. That means that you can choose how much you want to spend and how much time your ad will run. So, if you decide to pay $5 over the course of one day, Amazon will provide you statistics that will let you know how many people you will reach on average. You can adjust your budget or day limit to make use of the estimated number of clicks.

On average, a click costs no more than $0.35. That means that your advertisement will bring a potential customer to your shop for every $0.35 you spend. That is a fairly good average, and it is a great way to get exposure.

Self-Serve Ads vs. Premium Ads

If you perform a Google search, you will likely see two different kinds of ads; one is listed among the options in the Google results, and the other is listed in the banner on the side or bottom of the page. Self-serve ads are those that are listed with the results. So, if you find yourself looking for a product with keywords similar to those searched, the advertisements would be listed on that page.

On the other hand, premium ads are usually those that have photographs and are glaringly obvious during a search or in search results.

For example, if you search for hyena products, you will undoubtedly find many people with interesting views of hyenas, but you might also see an advertisement for Blow Pops listed on the side, tempting you.

Types of Amazon Ads

Though we have discussed the styles of ads you might see when creating an ad with Amazon, there are three main types that you can select when advertising with Amazon. Each accepts payments with different methods, and each should be used according to different marketing strategies.

Amazon Sponsored Product Ads

These are the most common types of ads not only on Amazon, but also on the internet.

Customers navigate to your page by finding products within a search. As discussed previously, these ads respond to keywords, phrases, and lines. They correspond with links to specific products.

If you are new to Amazon selling, you may want to start with this option. Remember, you sell products, not themes. Once you sell your product efficiently, you can move on to more products. Sponsor your product by searching for common keywords used in competitor sites. Once you have decided on the keywords that best describe your product and get the most traffic, set up your sponsored product ad accordingly.

When paying for a sponsored product ad, you must set a daily budget. Again, you may choose the money you wish to put into an ad, but be smart when considering how many people the ad will reach. For example, if you set a high budget for a single day, you may find that the day you selected is not the best to sell your merchandise. Setting up an ad to sell paint on a Tuesday may be less effective than doing it on Thursday, since more people are interested in home projects on the weekends. Allow the two-day shipping time for the product to reach your customer and decide which time is best to sell your product.

Headline Search Ads

Headline search ads are often associated with links to other sites or company pages. For example, you may see a headline search ad for a whisk-making company located at the top of a page with search results for kitchen supplies. These ads are often available for a date in the future, so you have time to organize your advertisement and subsequent product before it is released. Headline search ads are also keyword based, so you will not see an ad for a cucumber slicer on the same page as a security system unless you have an abstract way of protecting your home.

This ad is a pay-per-click, which means that every click on the ad costs the company money. These ads are known as campaigns and have a minimum budget of $0.10 per keyword. You must pay at least $100 to display these ads, and the minimum cost per day is $1.00.

When it comes to marketing, you would often use these types of ads to inspire others to visit your shop. This suggests that you have a brand already set up with a variety of options. Unlike the sponsored product ads, you may advertise for your whole inventory, so use this ad when you have built up a good backing. Since the prices for running one of these ads are generally higher, be prepared to shell out a decent amount of money to run it.

Amazon Product Display Ads

The final type of Amazon ad is the product display ad. Unlike the other two, customers are led to various products through other product detail pages. If you visit Amazon and select a product, you will notice that the ads listed on the page often offer products that are similar to the products or include similar interests. For example, a runner looking for ankle weights might find an ad for running shoes. Amazon uses interests and keywords selected from a long list of options to provide the perfect example for all customers.

Using this ad is a good marketing technique for both new and seasoned sellers. The best way to utilize this type of ad is to do market research on the most common interests and uses for products related to yours. However, since there is a potential list from which to choose, your market research need not be as intense.

Instead, take some time reviewing products that are similar to yours.

How to Optimize Amazon Ads

Like the product listings, it is necessary to optimize Amazon ads to get the most out of your money. Optimizing ads is slightly different than providing keywords for your products, but they do have remarkable similarities. For both, you want to utilize the tools on Amazon to find the best companies to emulate, but instead of placing all keywords in your ad, you must bid on the best keywords. Some keywords are used frequently, so they often cost more than less-used versions. Always be aware of the best ways to show your products. Below are six ways to optimize your Amazon ads and make selling that much easier.

Organize Campaigns

It may seem like a no-brainer that you must organize how you will submit your campaigns, but there is often more to it than meets the eye. For example, not only do you have to find the best times to produce your ads, but you also must find the best words to use in your campaign. This is commonly called an AdWords account structure. You define the words that would most benefit your campaign and use them in advertising.

Let us look at an example. If you own a business that specializes in cell phone sales, you may have three main categories: Apple, Samsung, and Motorola. These three categories can be broken down even further to specialize in each brand. The Apple Brand may break down into iPhone X, iPhone 8, and iPhone 7. Samsung might have subcategories that include the Galaxy Note10, Galaxy S10, and the Galaxy

A20. Motorola may be divided into subcategories such as Moto G, Moto Z, and Moto One. All of these phones have their own subcategories, which may include storage, RAM, etc.

The breakdown of each of these categories provides its own unique set of keywords that can be utilized in ads. Create several ads that support each keyword to get the most exposure.

You will see an increase in sales if you research how much each keyword is used in popular sites. Visit well-known company sites and do a keyword search. Though many company pages will have some of the same keywords, sift through these to find keywords that will match your ad.

Create Compelling and Urgent Ad Copy

No one wants to read about a product that simply explains why the seller thinks the product is so great. Though it is a good idea to include details in your copy, remember that people from all walks of life will be reading it. You want to be able to reach as many people as possible in as short a time as possible. People are more likely to click on a product if they do not have to slog through all the literature.

Though you want to reach as wide an audience as possible, marketing in too wide a market will often result in fewer clicks as your copy does not answer questions about the product. Keywords come back as a seller's best friend because the more specific you can become with your copy, the more likely people are to see what you have to say.

Create an urgent desire for your product. If you are selling shoe inserts, find out the problems most people have with their shoes and capitalize on them. Advertising a shoe insert as a solution to bad posture may not seem like the best option, but advertising that the insert will help to solve back problems will encourage customers to visit your product's page. People looking for solutions to problems are more likely to write down the symptom than the remedy when searching for products.

Create Specific Ads

We cannot stress enough that being specific in your product descriptions and ads is one of the best ways to create an ad that will stick in customer's minds. Most people do not search the web by typing "yellow" into a Google search window. Buyers are looking for specific solutions to their problems.

Keywords such as "phone" or "paint" may put you on a search list, but you will likely only have the spot on the 1,000th page. Instead, consider narrowing the search area by adding adjectives and adverbs. For example, key phrases like "16GB phone" or "primer paint" narrow down the search considerably.

Bid on Popular Brands

It may seem overwhelming to compete with big-name brands such as Maybelline or North Face, but you can use these brands to get ahead in the advertising game. For example, instead of using words like "furniture," select a large brand like "IKEA." Since these brands are often at the top of lists, it is more likely that your brand name will appear with the big dogs.

If you have a rather specific niche and are looking for the top competitors for more unique items, simply type a general term into a search engine. The results will yield ads from other companies (good signs that they have enough cash flow to afford ads on Google searches) and you will likely find articles that rank the best brand names in the biz.

Experiment with Ad Formats

Though we have specified which marketing technique works with each of the brands, do not be afraid to experiment. In fact, spend your marketing time doing just that. Though it may seem as though product sponsored ads are the only way to go when marketing for the first time, try a different option and compare the results. You may find that you like one version over the other.

The different ad formats reach shoppers in different ways. For example, though some like to find the ads at the top of their list of results, others may find it more helpful to find another product by clicking on an ad within the product details. Use your experience and survey others to see what they look for in an ad.

Use Negative Keywords

Negative keywords prevent buyers from viewing your ad because it does not match the keyword. For example, if you were to sell hummingbird homes and someone searched for home interior, they may see your ad, which would be a waste of a click. Your ads are only shown to so many people, depending on your budget and time frame. To prevent this from happening, use negative keywords to prevent accidental clicks. You may choose the word "kitchen" or "bedroom" to exclude any searches that may contain those keywords.

Often, when you use negative keywords, you are inadvertently also preventing your products from showing up in large, generic searches, which may also save you a view. The ads you optimize through this method often are marketed for specific results, so choose your negative keywords wisely.

Conclusion

Amazon ads are some of the best utilized in the business, and since you are now a fully-fledged Amazon seller, take advantage of some of the best technology out there. Consider what you can do when you stake a place for yourself in one of the world's leading online shopping companies.

If you are concerned about whether you should advertise with Amazon ads, the answer is still a resounding yes! Not only could you get more bang for your buck by launching ads specific to your products, but you will also gain much-needed exposure. Remember that your products are only as valuable as you make them, so give them the star treatment.

There are three types of Amazon ads: sponsored product ads, headline search ads, and Amazon product display ads. Each is unique in its opportunity to reach several types of audiences. If you feel as though you are going to break the bank with this venture, do not worry. You can often choose the amount of money you want to spend on each ad and select the right time frame for you.

Optimizing ads, just like optimizing your products, is one of the most beneficial ways to encourage new customers to see your products. Make sure your ads are organized or you will never know which ads perform well for which products. Organize your ads into keyword research, and apply two or more ads to every subcategory to find out which type of ad works best. Remember, do not be afraid to experiment.

Be specific in your ads, and bring in the use of other brand names to make your brand pop. Even though you may not sell North Face jackets, you can always market your products as items similar to them. These specific keywords associated with big brands also narrow down the amount of general information customers have to sift through in order to find your product. The use of negative keywords also helps to prevent general terms from using your clicks.

Chapter 11: Creating Your Brand

Now that you have completed the setup and are on your way to creating a store that will be the envy of all other stores, the bulk of the hard work is done. All right, so the hard work is maintaining a profitable store on Amazon, but you have completed everything necessary for an excellent startup. The rest of the work comes through making your business stand the test of time.

Monitoring Your Amazon FBA Business

Even if you have automated the rest of your store, it is still necessary to make sure that everything is still in working order while you wander the beaches of the Bahamas. Below is a list of the most important parts of your business to monitor after you have completed the majority of the work.

Earnings

Though you may have found your time to shine in the halls of the Amazon FBA elite, you still need to regularly check your earnings. If you see the numbers start to slip, add more market research to your routine. Amazon has a detailed list of payment reports that are available to every Amazon FBA seller, so check the record frequently to see where you stand.

Fees

Though often thought of as the bane of the business existence, they are still a very active part of what you earn. If you notice an increase in fees, check your emails to find an Amazon email that will explain the change. Always remember that fees are subject to change at any time, and storage fees jump to more than three times the normal rate from October through December. Change your prices according to the changes in fees to allow for more profitable results.

Seller Rank

It is not enough to be a seller; you have to be the best seller on Amazon. Okay, so this can go too far in many ways, but always remember that your seller rank determines your profits. As you continue to grow your business, always strive to climb the ladder to become the best in your niche.

Also remember to score well with customers. Always respond to questions unanswered and make it a point to connect with your customers. Your overall rank will increase when customers are satisfied with your products.

Order Defect Rate

Always monitor the products that you send to the public. If you consistently send products that are damaged or otherwise impaired, you may suffer from a loss of understanding from Amazon. Amazon has been known to delete listings due to inferior products.

Perfect Order Percentage

This is mostly out of your hands since Amazon handles all the shipping and handling after you send them the product, but it is important to maintain a high percentage by keeping all inventory in stock and following up on orders that have been lost. If you receive a large percentage of lost packages, speak with Amazon and request information about the losses.

Customer Dissatisfaction Rate

The customers are your greatest asset when dealing with Amazon FBA. You want to make sure that they are happy with their products and will come back again and again. If you work within a commingling account, your dissatisfaction rate may increase due to other sellers who offer cheap products. Always stay a cut above the game by ensuring your customers are getting the right product by letting them know which brand to choose.

Pre-Fulfillment Cancellation Rate

The pre-fulfillment cancellation rate is completed by the seller who usually does not have enough inventory in stock. To prevent this from happening, always maintain a constant stream of stock headed to Amazon at all times. Amazon is very unforgiving when it comes to a low pre-fulfillment cancellation rate and only accepts a 2.5% window of failure. To find your rate, divide the number of orders you have canceled by the number of total products sold.

Conversion Rate

See how much your customer base changes over time by seeing how the numbers fluctuate between your store and others with similar products. Also, discover your conversion rate by comparing days, months, or weeks. Always use the same time period when calculating rates.

Conclusion

When starting your business, it is a good idea to get the most fundamental things out of the way, but when you are finished, it is important to keep an eye on your business to see where it is and is not growing. Be prepared to follow competitors and continue with your marketing every day to become a better seller with Amazon FBA. It is your responsibility to take care of your business, so make it a priority.

Take care to understand how your information is running from the most menial detail to the bigger picture. The only way to profit from your company is to keep an eye on your financials. This means that you must monitor your earnings every day. From fee deductions to loss of inventory, you need to know that you can still make a profit on the products you sell. Fees often sneak up on sellers if you do not know all of the fees involved. Refresh the fee policies often to make sure you understand all changes.

Though you do not have complete control over your seller rank, you must constantly monitor every comment made about your products to improve and build customer trust. Look to obtain a nearly perfect order percentage. If you forget about the products that need stocking, ask a third-party company to do the majority of the work for you. Though it may cost extra to get the best service, it may be worth it.

Make sure that customers understand when you are trying to fix an issue, and often communicate your apologies to customers who have received defective products. Your customers are the people that keep you in business, so monitor how you well you retain those customers. Be vocal and active with your products.

Conclusion

Amazon is one of the leading companies of online stores in the world, and it is easy to see why: They have products that many customers did not know they needed, and it is usually at an unbeatable price. Since its beginning, Amazon has been completely devoted to its loyal customer base, and it has only expanded the savings for loyal customers by offering incentives such as Amazon Prime.

With all the sales that Amazon generates every month, it only makes sense to take a part of that pie. After all, if anyone can learn this, you can. Third-party sellers make up more than half of the selling companies on Amazon, and they command a whopping three times the number of products. There is always room for more products in Amazon's massive warehouse collection, and you should be one of the many sellers who can make a living from selling products.

So, do you have what it takes? If you completed this book, then it is obvious that you do. The most difficult part of Amazon FBA is becoming a motivated seller that can take the frustration that may come from sales (or lack thereof) and turn it around. Even if you believe that this does not describe you, we promise that you can get there. All it takes is a little elbow grease and a lot of heart.

Why would you want to sign up with Amazon FBA when there are other options out there and you are just starting out? Amazon has created a third-party selling model that has inspired thousands of other businesses, and they have only refined their practices, so you know that you are getting the most out of the business.

Developing a mindset that will propel you through the most difficult times in your seller journey is absolutely vital. Luckily, we proved that you can find motivation in anything, even setbacks. Find only the best information on the internet and books and sift through the stuff that either makes you waste your time or ends up completely wrong. Believe us, we have seen both sides of that equation. As soon as you find your center with the right information, you can start to build your vision through careful planning and goals. Create your vision from your passions, and it will become easier to be motivated in the future. Once you have set up your goals, keep at them and renew them every time they expire. If you do not meet the goal you had hoped, try again. There is no expiration date for success.

Amazon is responsible for the majority of the work in your professional relationship, which frees up your time to do the things necessary to grow your business. As soon as you send your products to Amazon, they file your products away in a warehouse awaiting a customer. As soon as there is a bite, they send your product to the customer, all of which is done with the Prime shipping plan. Customers get two-day shipping and you get the peace of mind knowing that you did not have to do anything else. Amazon is in charge of customer service and your payment, and all you have to do is keep that inventory stocked for more customers.

Just as with any other company, there are advantages and disadvantages to working with Amazon FBA. If you like the idea of selling but do not want to handle all the customer interaction that goes with it, Amazon FBA is an excellent choice for you. They also offer discounted shipping rates for their professional account holders, which means you can ship packages to Amazon much cheaper than it would cost for you to send them out yourself. Amazon also manages all returns and customer complaints unless there is something wrong with the product. Amazon has potentially unlimited storage space (if you have the money to keep all of it stocked) and promises quick delivery to and from the Amazon warehouse. Amazon also includes a multi-channel fulfillment option that allows you to sell products from your own site.

However, if you are struggling with finances, the costs and fees are difficult to overcome, especially if your products simply sit on the shelves, not budging. Because Amazon promises free returns, you may also have to pay a fee for all customer returns, which can add up. When you create an account, you may have to handle difficult product preparation including obtaining a UPC code and handling all packaging. You are also responsible for the sales tax you receive from your sales. Though Amazon takes the taxes for you, they require that you pay them to all the states necessary, which can get hairy. Finally, commingling can be dangerous if you are not careful. Be sure to work with a company that offers quality products to prevent returns and bad customer reviews.

Set up a seller account with either an individual or a professional account. We recommend the individual account if you are just starting to sell with Amazon. If you are more accustomed to selling, take the plunge with a professional account. Not only will you receive more benefits, but you do not have to worry about Amazon's $1.00 fee for every product purchased. Remember to read all sections of your profile account to find the best information and change the wrong information before you start to sell to prevent a future headache.

When discovering the product that is perfect for you, remember that there is no such thing as a perfect product. Just choose a lucrative product and start selling! Engage your audience, friends, and family with surveys about products you would like to sell or those you have already sold. It is important to use the best information when setting up your own shop to prevent you from squandering your money on non-profitable products. Check out online resources to find a profitable product and then stick to it! You can grow your empire when you have mastered a single product.

Find your niche by looking through the products you are passionate about. If you find yourself passionate about more than one thing, use that information to better sell your product and move on to the next one. Avoid products that go in and out of season and instead settle for products that are useful and profitable all year long. Grow your marketing by creating videos and reviews for your products. Remember that the best products are those that are smaller because they are easier to handle and store. Create a place where you can search for your niche and enjoy the process.

Whether you choose wholesalers, overseas merchants, or a little bit of both, gain an understanding with your providers and open the lines of communication. Be an advocate for your product and the people with whom you work. Use your negotiation skills to find the best products at the best prices.

Create an optimized listing and ad by becoming aware of the product's features and dimensions. Instead of just putting yourself in your customer's shoes, put your customers in your shoes. Give them enough detail that they will know exactly what they need to know about the product. They can always ask you more questions later, but get as much detail onto the platform as possible. Use the ads within Amazon to guide customers to your site. You can use sponsored product ads, headline search ads, or product display ads, but do not just stop at one. Use all of your options to find out which one works for you.

Finally, always remember to monitor your account. Pay attention to your finances and always remember to put the customer first. They are the people that bring you success, and you should treat them like it.

With all the knowledge you have learned about Amazon FBA, do not be afraid to try out your own ideas and become the best seller on Amazon.

References

10 key metrics FBA businesses should monitor. (2017, November 9). Retrieved from https://www.forecast.ly/11-key-metrics-fba-businesses-monitor/

Amazon. (n.d.-a). Amazon Fulfillment: Our fulfillment centers. Retrieved from https://www.aboutamazon.com/amazon-fulfillment/our-fulfillment-centers/

Amazon. (n.d.-b). FBA fulfillment fees for Amazon.com orders. Retrieved from https://sellercentral.amazon.com/gp/help/external/201112670?language=en_US&ref=efph_201112670_cont_G201112630

Amazon. (n.d.-c). Multi-channel fulfillment - Amazon.com. Retrieved from https://services.amazon.com/fulfillment-by-amazon/multi-channel.html

Amazon. (2019, December 9). News and updates on Fulfillment by Amazon (FBA) - Amazon.com. Retrieved from https://services.amazon.com/fulfillment-by-amazon/news-and-updates.html

Arishekar, N. (2019, August 1). Top 9 ways to find profitable Amazon niche product. Retrieved from https://www.sellerapp.com/blog/find-amazon-niche/

Bond, C. (2019, August 27). A complete guide to fulfillment by Amazon (FBA). Retrieved from https://www.wordstream.com/blog/ws/2018/09/19/amazon-fba

Buy Box. (2019, October 31). Create an Amazon seller central account. Retrieved from https://www.buyboxexperts.com/create-an-amazon-seller-central-account/

Carragher, G. (2018, December 13). How to leverage the power of Amazon FBA. Retrieved from https://www.bigcommerce.com/blog/amazon -fba/#14-tactics-to-successfully-sell-on- amazon-fba

Chou, S. (n.d.). FBA calculator - Hidden fees all Amazon sellers should know about. Retrieved from https://mywifequitherjob.com/amazon- fba-fee- calculator/#Is_Amazon_FBA_A_Ripoff

Dayton, E. (2019, May 18). Amazon statistics you should know: Opportunities to make the most of America's top online marketplace. Retrieved from https://www.bigcommerce.com/blog/amazon -statistics/#10-fascinating-amazon-statistics- sellers-need-to-know-in-2019

DePillis, L., & Sherman, I. (2019, July 5). Amazon's extraordinary 25-year evolution.

Retrieved from https://edition.cnn.com/interactive/2018/10/business/amazon-history-timeline/index.html

Dunn, J. (2019, January 13). Amazon FBA sales tax guide for 2019. Retrieved from https://www.bigcommerce.com/blog/amazon-fba-sales-tax/#undefined

Farese, D. (2019, November 7). How to do market research: A 6-step guide. Retrieved from https://blog.hubspot.com/marketing/market-research-buyers-journey-guide

Grant, R. (2019, April 9). How to buy wholesale to sell on Amazon FBA in 2019. Retrieved from https://onlinesellingexperiment.com/wholesale-amazon-intro/

Gregory, S. (2019, April 16). 11 simple steps for a successful brand building process. Retrieved from https://freshsparks.com/successful-brand-building-process/

Masters, K. (2018, June 21). Amazon revolutionized order fulfillment, but this company is creating Prime-like shipping for all. Retrieved from https://www.forbes.com/sites/kirimasters/2018/06/21/amazon-revolutionized-order-fulfillment-but-this-company-is-creating-prime-like-shipping-for-all/#55109aa46a5a

Mercer, G. (2019, October 15). The 6 pillars of Amazon product listing optimization. Retrieved from https://startupbros.com/6-amazon-product-listing-optimization/

Mercer, Greg. (2018, September 4). Amazon FBA fees explained - The ultimate guide. Retrieved from https://www.junglescout.com/blog/amazon-fba-fees/

Mitchell, W. (2019a, August 1). Step-by-step guide: How to find a profitable product to sell. Retrieved from https://startupbros.com/step-by-step-guide-on-how-to-find-a-profitable-product-to-sell/

Mitchell, W. (2019b, October 15). How to sell on Amazon: The ultimate beginner's guide to your business. Retrieved from https://startupbros.com/how-to-sell-on-amazon-fba/

Smale, T. (2016, March 23). 5 steps you can use to find your niche. Retrieved from https://www.entrepreneur.com/article/27280 8

TaxJar. (2016, June 14). Sales Tax Guide for Amazon FBA Sellers. Retrieved from https://www.taxjar.com/guides/sales-tax-guide-for-amazon-fba/#determining-sales-tax-nexus

Thum, M. (2008, July 3). How to change limiting beliefs. Retrieved from http://www.myrkothum.com/how-to-change-self-limiting-beliefs/

Thum, M. (2012, November 26). The right mindset: change your mindset in 6 steps. Retrieved from https://www.myrkothum.com/mindset/

WebFX, Inc. (n.d.). 4 Amazon seller metrics you must monitor for success. Retrieved from https://www.webfx.com/amazon/amazon-seller-metrics.html

Whitney, M. (2019, August 27). Complete beginner's guide to marketing on Amazon. Retrieved from https://www.wordstream.com/blog/ws/2017/09/11/amazon-advertising

Passive Income Ideas 2020

The Best Strategies and Secrets to Make Money from Home and Reach Financial Freedom - Amazon FBA, Dropshipping, Affiliate Marketing, Kindle Publishing, Blogging and More

Disclaimer Notice:

Please note the information contained within this document is for educational and entertainment purposes only. All effort has been executed to present accurate, up to date, and reliable, complete information. No warranties of any kind are declared or implied. Readers acknowledge that the author is not engaging in the rendering of legal, financial, medical or professional advice. The content within this book has been derived from various sources. Please consult a licensed professional before attempting any techniques outlined in this book.

By reading this document, the reader agrees that under no circumstances is the author responsible for any losses, direct or indirect, which are incurred as a result of the information contained within this document, including, but not limited to, — errors, omissions, or inaccuracies.

Introduction

Money. We all need it to live in this modern day world. How much importance you attach to it is your own concern. However, it can't be denied that money can improve our quality of life and standard of living. Otherwise, why do we get up and go to work every day? For fun? Maybe. For the majority of us, work is a means to survival, and to a better life. It brings us the comfort of steady income. However, for most of us, a steady paying job is not enough for us to achieve our lifelong goals and live out our dreams. It may not even provide the financial stability that you need.

What are the solutions? Should we take on another job? Maybe you can. Maybe you have. Maybe your job is too straining, and the additional load will be too much. There may not be enough hours in the day for you to be in a position to do something like this.

This is where passive income can play an important role in your life. Irrespective of your circumstances, or your financial status, obtaining a passive income can drive you to greater heights financially, giving you more economic freedom and the platform with which you can achieve your goals.

What is Passive Income?

Currently, if you're employed, you are earning an active income. An active income is any income where you are required to have a direct and continuous involvement in the generation of income. If you don't go to work, you probably don't make any money for that day. That is the basis of active income.

Passive income, on the other hand, is the money that you can earn with minimal and indirect upkeep. With time, passive income can generate regular and sustainable income that will build over time. Besides, of course, the fact that you are bringing in more money, there are many benefits to acquiring a passive income (Wanderlust Worker, 2019).

For one, I'm sure you'll be aware that the increased income will give you a much more stress-free environment. You may find yourself deep in debt to pay your bills and fearing future outcomes. Here, you will find passive income will help to lessen your fears as you have will always have a backup solution; a viable option to fall back on should you find yourself in a crisis. You'll have more energy to invest in your days ahead, free from the what-ifs and thoughts of financial collapse.

With this, we can see another one of the many benefits of passive income: freedom. Given that you are not active in the work you are pursuing, this will give you something truly valuable in life, that many of us take for granted: time. You will have the time to do the things that you find enjoyable. If you're a parent, you'll have more valuable time to spend with your kids, giving them the attention that you may not have been able to before.

Maybe, like me, you have a desire to see the world in all its beauty, and with a passive income, you have the benefit of being able to be anywhere in the world, and still have the ability to work on your income from there. In our day to day lives, we probably plan a holiday way in advance, and then have to wait several more years before we have the ability to plan the next one. With a reliable passive income, you can transcend these boundaries, and travel however much it suits you. Remember that word: freedom. Freedom to do the things we love, with the people we love, and engage in all of the enjoyment that life has to offer.

With that being said, if there are all these lovely benefits stuff centered around passive income, why have you not heard much about it? Well, the truth is, you probably have, but maybe you weren't paying enough attention at the time. In the other sense, that it doesn't look to be popular, is that there appears to be several rather misguided theories to the idea of passive income. One of the most common of them is that you need money to start generating passive income. While some ideas may require an initial startup fee, many require little to no money; merely your initiative to work at it and be consistent.

The other theory I find bandied about is that you need to have a great business idea in order to start making extra income. Venturing into passive income does not require you to become an entrepreneur, but instead rely on tried and trusted ideas that have been used over and over again to build wealth. Some can be as boring as opening up a retirement or savings account that generates extra money over time. Boring, but certainly effective.

Once you do get started, it should be noted that this is NOT an overnight process. You're not suddenly going to create a website or investment in stocks and see returns the next day. Although it was mentioned earlier that they require little to no upkeep, the process of starting up will require you to be consistent and dedicated in your approach to growing your income. Take the time to learn what about the industries you decide to involve yourself in, so that you may be prepared for any trials and challenges that lay ahead. Nothing in life is achieved without some degree of effort, and this is no different.

Within this book, you will find a few different ways to look into developing your passive income, the ins and outs of each type of income and how you could possibly go about getting started. From here, you will be able to achieve a rough guideline into what choices would be available and suitable to your situation, skills and even lifestyle.

Let's dive right in!

Chapter 1: The Right Mind for Your Business

Starting up a business is by no means an easy feat. With that in mind, before we get started, it's important to ensure that you have an idea of what and why it is you would like to start a business. First off, you need to enter the field with the right mindset. Arguably, the mindset is one of the most vital aspects in starting your business, and taking on the challenges that follow in time. So, within this chapter, we will look at the various aspects of being a business owner, and what you need to get started on the right track. In many ways, developing and maintaining a passive income is a form of business. You are creating an avenue for yourself to make money, relying solely on your planning, logic and self-discipline in order to continually build up your income.

One of the important traits to have when getting started, is patience. Planning your own business with the expectation of an immediate return, is unrealistic and will leave you feeling shattered and disappointed. You must be prepared to understand that the goal is longevity, and not immediate wealth. If you were looking for ways to create immediate wealth, I would suggest playing the lottery, or heading to the tables or slot machines at your nearest casinos. What are the chances of your success there? Minimal, if not at all. Playing the long game ensures that you are building a steady and reliable source of income, that will benefit you over the long term, while minimizing risk and, if done the right way, maximizing your rewards (The Human Factor, 2019).

A key mistake, that goes hand in hand with this, is that people will look at a field they have no interest in, because they think it will make them rich. Choosing a field that leaves you feeling satisfied provides a sense of accomplishment and gives you an enjoyment in what it is you are doing. If you find yourself having no pleasure out of the activity, you will probably not pay as much attention to it, as you would had it been something that you did enjoy, and in the end, you will most likely set it aside for something better. When getting started, ask yourself if it is something if the idea you have chosen is something you are passionate about; something that you would enjoy doing. If you find it is not, move on to something that you would. If you didn't like an idea, then it probably wasn't for you. Don't see it as a loss of an option, but instead as an opportunity for something better.

That last statement is critical in developing your business. Remaining positive, and seeing a silver lining in all aspects of the business that you may encounter is powerful. Over the course of your venture into passive income, you may find yourself facing several different challenges that will threaten to bring you down. As an example, maybe you've taken a heavy loss or you've not been able to successfully attract the market to your business for a long time. These would probably be enough to bring anybody down. However, you have to find yourself rising above the idea of falling into despair, or giving up entirely. Failure in business, is most likely going to be an inevitability.

Listen to any successful CEO tell his or her story, and somewhere along the line you will hear about a moment where he or she made mistakes and hit a few stumbling blocks. Treat every moment in failure as a learning venture, and a chance to address your business, so that the same cannot occur again. In this case, you've done something to improve the business and ensure its chances of success. Everything is an opportunity to be better, and this is entirely how you should look at the concept of business. Failure is when we quit. Mistakes are when we learn.

Another mistake one can inevitably make, is not having a plan. If you find yourself heading into a business idea without a plan, a goal, or even an idea of why you started attempting to create a passive income in the first place, you're not going to go very far. A plan then, in this case, is not knowing every step that you are going to take, how much money you will make in five years or how successful your business will be in ten years. Those are merely expectations, and should your business not reach those heights, you will feel naturally disappointed.

A plan starts with the necessary and extensive research into your chosen industry, determining your target market and how you will plan to engage with that market. This would also include planning your finances and cost for anything you may need. Essentially, what you are doing is setting up a plan on how your business is going to start. From there, you can set goals, but they should be based on yourself, not on the market or your expectations of success. For example, if you would like to become a YouTuber, you can start by setting yourself a goal of doing one video every week, or more or less, depending on your own schedule. This way, we can ensure that our goals are being met in from the beginning, and we can feel a sense of accomplishment from what we are doing.

However, this should not stop one from thinking ahead. As a business owner, you need to always be one step ahead. Now, I did not say five or six steps ahead earlier, as mentioned before, because the future is unpredictable. Just a single step. This step is enough to help you to assess the market for your business and adjust accordingly. Take action when it's necessary, not when you feel ready, and don't let outside factors influence the decisions that you will make.

When we are getting started in business, impulsiveness should be one of the furthest things from our way of thinking. Everything will require strategic planning and an understanding of the business as a whole. From there, you can see your business realistically and move forward with this in mind.

Take Responsibility

So far, we have looked at how positivity and a learning mentality is vital in moving your business forward. The mind is arguably one of the most important aspects in creating a business, and will often decide how far you can take it. You can start by insuring that you believe in both yourself, and the business that you are trying to build. This allows you to dedicate yourself fully to the plan you have in mind. As for believing in yourself, having a business idea that plays to your strengths rather than your weaknesses gives you a firm grasp on the tasks on hand. A business that incorporates several of your weaknesses can become a chore and will make you feel listless and frustrated. These are not feelings we want to associate in the business we are developing.

Alongside this, as you are the one solely in charge; you need to be the one to hold yourself accountable. Take responsibility for the paths that you take, and know that the buck stops with you. Nothing is out of your control, and whenever a decision needs to be made, you need to be the one to take action. After all, this is your business. If you do not nurture it, who else is going to do so? Failing to hold yourself accountable, will result in a failure to learn, and a failure to learn will result in a negative pattern that you build for yourself, moving in a cycle around the same mistakes.

So, remember - positivity, determination, acceptance of the idea of failure and accountability are what makes for a successful business venture.

Looking Ahead

Throughout your life, you will encounter people discussing this 'fantastic' business idea they have, or how they've begun to create and develop their own business. Most of the time, the idea is never acted upon, or the business that was being created fades into oblivion, never to be mentioned again. Usually, due to a culmination of the above or a fear to take the plunge into a world they don't quite understand. Starting something on your own takes a lot of guts, and from time to time, you must be willing to take calculated risks. Notice that I say **calculated** risk. If you find yourself taking risks without assessing them properly, you're just playing the lottery all over again. Taking care to ensure that the outcome of the risk is tolerable for both you and your business' needs.

Throughout your business venture, you will need all the skills we have looked at in continuing to ensure that your venture is a worthwhile success. From the startup to an ever-changing and overly dynamic market, to economic 'drama' and unplanned setbacks. You will face a multitude of unforeseen challenges. The key is how you learn, adapt and move past these boundaries in the best manner possible for you. From there, you build the roads that will take you further.

From here, we will move into several unique and creative ways of developing a passive income that you can potentially use to start your journey. Remember to consider your own strengths and weaknesses to judge what would be most applicable to you, as well as your financial status and the interest you have in said field. Look at what you are passionate about and how they will associate with the passive incomes that we will head through. I now leave it all up to you to make the right choice for yourself.

Chapter 2: Dropshipping

Dropshipping is the business model whereby a retail inventory, store or traditional retail arrangement is not required. Instead, the retail company sells the product available, and the order is then transferred to a third-party; a supplier who then delivers the product to the customer. In other words, you sell products that you don't have to stock, ship or even touch. Your drop-shipping supplier does that for you.

Over time, like many of the examples in this book, dropshipping has seen a significant rise in popularity, as it looks to streamline the process in which products are sold and delivered online (Shopify, 2019). In 2017, dropshipping saw a growing market emerge, with approximately 23% percent of all online sales completed via dropshipping, and as time wears on, with the eCommerce market expanding rapidly, it will continue to grow in new and exciting ways.

Irwin Dominguez, is one of the many who saw this emerging market, and looked to take advantage of it, going from zero to **millions** in sales in less than twelve months! An online marketing consultant, Irwin decided to test out the industry after hearing of its success from a friend. After some research, he opened a Shopify account, created a store before adding a few products with Oberlo. With a little marketing and advertising, his business, with little to no capital, blew up in months, and now generates on average around $10,000 per day! (Crazylister.com, 2019)

Another story I am particularly fond of is that of a woman named Kate. It isn't any kind of rags-to-riches story, or a story about neverending struggles on her way to success.

There is nothing really extraordinary about it. That is, in fact, what I like about it.

What is great about this story, is that Kate took something that she had her own personal interest in; in this case, anime (Japanese comics). She took something that she was passionate about, and turned it into something valuable for herself. In this case, netting $32,000 in monthly revenue.

All sounds great, doesn't it? Some entrepreneur makes several thousands of dollars per day not long after starting his business and it's happily ever after? Not quite. I do not want you to go into this process believing that this is a get rich quick scheme. Dropshipping takes a lot of dedication, hard work and planning to be successful, and no two company success stories are the same. Whereas Irwin built his fortune in a few months, some take years and years to really build a customer base to which they can sell these products. Each market is different, and going in expecting instant rewards will disappoint. Change your mindset. Go into the field with the goal of learning, instead of making money, and see and plan out your rise to success from there.

So now that you've heard a little about what dropshipping is, and a few stories of success, let's look at why dropshipping is an attractive industry to move into. Aside from the growing eCommerce market, dropshipping provides you with more flexibility and freedom. You don't have to own a large warehouse, or store products for sales. You don't even need to be in the same country! The business model is fairly easy to grasp, and the startup costs are minimal. With all this, you are offered financial and personal flexibility with which to plan your life between business and pleasure. There are also plenty of helpful tools that you can use to help you when getting started in the dropshipping industry, which is what we will look at now.

Starting Your Own Dropshipping Business.

So you've decided that dropshipping is the option for you, and that this will place you on the journey to reliable passive income. Well, I'm here to help! Throughout this, remember that you are building a brand that represents you. And just like personal growth, we want this brand to reach as high as it possibly can.

Choosing A Niche

The first thing you're going to do is think of the market that you would like to attract. While it's possible to sell just about anything and everything through your store, this will create a cluster of confusion as to what it is that you are offering, and you will struggle to attract a target market. Developing a niche for your business will give you the ability to reach a certain market with your products, and help you build up a client base. So, brainstorm a few ideas. Use your interests, and your hobbies to guide you here. Remember that we're more likely to be successful if it is something we are passionate about. Research more about your chosen field. Find out what people are interested in and where. Look at social media outlets such as Facebook, Instagram, etc. Are there groups that you could use to engage with others as well as share the products that you would like to sell? Of course! You just have to find them!

Once you have decided on a niche, and that there is an established market for it, it is now time to find a supplier for your products. Again, a search engine is your friend here. There are a great deal of online suppliers available, each with their own pros and cons. Dig deep into their websites to determine if the products they offer are suitable for the demands of those you are looking to sell to. As soon as you find the supplier you feel is the best fit, get in touch with them, and find out if they dropship their products, as well as what their requirements are, so that you can negotiate the best deal possible for yourself.

Deciding On A Brand

Now it's time for you to establish your brand. This will define your business, and will guide you into the decisions you will make for your store in the future. Think of all the most popular brands. Think of those that you favor when you purchase something. They invoke a feeling within you. That's how that brand has positioned itself to make you feel.Your brand will be what sets you apart from the others, and why customers will come to you instead.

You'll need a name to start. We don't want to overcomplicate here. Again, think of the best brands. It's simple, short and precise, sliding off the tongue. Try to consider a brand name that is short and easy to say, but will set you apart from the rest.

To go with your brand name, you'll need a slogan. A tagline, in other words. Again, aim to keep it short but catchy.

The final piece of presentation of your brand, is the logo. This will merge with the name and slogan, to create a graphic and hopefully memorable representation of your brand.

Seems like a lot to take in, doesn't it? In reality, this is a simple process that just requires a little creativity. Only one thing left to do for now, and that is to develop a brand story. If you've ever visited a brand website, you'll have noticed an 'About Us' page. This is where you detail into a company's brand story. A brand story is there to inspire an emotional feeling in its audience. Brand stories give your clients something they feel they can associate with, and a reason to stand by your business over others.

Your brand story should define the purpose of your business, and will encompass your merchandise, social media platforms and advertisements. If clients can identify with your brand story, they will buy from you.

Congratulations! You have now created your very own brand!

The Marketplace

Now that you have a supplier and established your very own brand, it is time to set up your online store. There are several eCommerce platforms that will help you along through this, however I would suggest that you use Shopify to set up your store. Shopify offers you a 14-day free trial before commencing with a paid option. The store is very user-friendly and does not require you to have any sort of web development skills in order to create your store.

Within the parameters provided, you can use a variety of tools to make your store suitable to your brand as well aesthetically pleasing to any who may come across it. Don't overthink this, as you'll end up obsessing over it. You can make alterations and improvements to your store over time. The goal for now is to make your store look appealing and interesting to your customers, while allowing it to emphasize the products that you are selling.

Now that you've created your store, it's time to determine what products you will sell. I mentioned niche markets earlier. Keep that in mind now, and structure the products you are selling according to your niche. Make sure to categorize your website, so that clients are able to easily find what they are looking for. Alongside your products, you will have to determine the prices that they will sell for. You will eventually need to fork out a little cash when advertising your products, so keep this in mind when you are determining a price for your products. Try to aim for at least 30% gross profit on each item, if possible.

The final step here is to create your product page. This is the page of your store where clients can view the selected products and it's details.Try to create your own descriptions that entice the customer to buy the product. Remember that in some ways, your store is your salesman.

Once that is done, you've just about completed building your own dropshipping business. Remember that our website should have an 'About Us' page, an 'FAQ Page,' as well as 'Contact Us, Shipping, Refunds and Returns' pages and finally a "Privacy Policy and TOC's" page.

Now you have chosen your niche, established a brand, found your products and created a store. What do we do next? Well, launch, of course! Give yourself a pat on the back. You now run your very own business!

Advertising

The journey we have is far from over. You have a store, but how will people be able to find it? It is time for you to start promoting your store. For starters, you can use your own social media to let others know that you have launched. In turn, you should have already created numerous social media accounts for your business, so that clients have an easy path to finding it as well as communication.

Facebook is the most popular social network in the world, so it makes sense to use them to market your product. Facebook Ads can be a great way to market your products to a select group according to the criteria you determine, such as age, gender, location, etc. This is the first form of advertising you should start with. From there, you may advertise how you see fit.

Don't forget that ads or any other form of marketing is how you will bring clients to your store, so it needs to be appealing and persuasive. It is arguable the biggest aspect of building your client base.

Where To From Here?

Your business is now operating. You have a steady flow of income. So everything is done and dusted, right? You can just sit back and relax? Well, not quite. That is a mistake that I imagine many make. Industries and markets and forever changing. It is your job to monitor these changes and move with them. If your products are no longer selling, it's time to look at alternatives that you think will sell. This can be avoided if you always keep your store up to date according to the latest trends. Make sure that you interact with your customer base. Give them an opportunity to leave reviews of both products *and* services, and engage with them if they are not happy about something.

Don't be an apathetic businessman, otherwise you will find yourself losing business. Remember to be consistent in improvement. If you do not try to improve, your store will stagnate, and that will hinder its growth. Be ambitious. If you constantly strive to improve, you will find yourself reaching higher peaks and taking your business further.

Maybe you will become the next success story that we will read about!

Chapter 3: Amazon FBA

Amazon is widely considered to be the world's largest eCommerce company, according to revenue. They have invested themselves into several aspects of eCommerce, with one of those aspects being Amazon FBA.

Fulfillment by Amazon (FBA) is a service that provides storage, packaging and shipping assistance to sellers. Unlike dropshipping, where you do not own any merchandise, Amazon FBA has you invest in merchandise that is then stored at one of their warehouses. The products are packed and shipped, all courtesy of Amazon.

This works to your benefit, as you have the credibility of Amazon being associated with your products, and customers will feel they are more likely to receive quality products through your business. On top of this, you will never have to handle any merchandise, which can take the burden off of handling and maneuvering large volumes of equipment. Using Amazon FBA also means that you will pay lower shipping fees, due to their relationships with certain shipping companies.

As I am sure you have already guessed, using Amazon's services will cost you a bit of money. Amazon will take approximately 15% of your product price once it is sold, along with storage, shipping and handling fees that you will have to pay.

Now you may be thinking that dropshipping is already a better alternative, as you avoid having to pay several fees, however each comes with its own perks according to your business model.

With dropshipping, you are required to build up a client base in order to sell your product. However, Amazon allows you to bypass some of this, as you have access to their huge customer base, while increasing your profit margins due to a higher selling price, courtesy, again, of the Amazon brand.

Naturally, you will have doubts about involving any of the giant-size brands in your startup business, such as Amazon, there is much success to be made from this kind of business model. Amazon FBA's profit margins and branching revenue streams make it possible to greatly increase the earning potential for your business.

Spencer Haws, owner of Niche Pursuits, used this to his advantage, selling his products on Amazon and raking in approximately $40,000 dollars in his first month. This just shows that there is tremendous potential for profits within the industry, just in merely finding the right niche. The possibilities that await are potentially endless!

Building Your Amazon FBA Business

So now that you're interested in starting your own Amazon FBA business, where do you actually begin?

Open an account and consider your niche

Well, the first step is to open a 'Seller Account' with Amazon. You can either opt for a Professional or an Individual account. The Individual account does not require any monthly subscription, however you will have several limitations placed on your account. These could work for you, or against you, depending on the needs of your business.

Just as you would do in dropshipping, you will need to find a niche for your business. Remember to relate it to something that you're interested in, such as a hobby or special interest. Don't throw away extra ideas you may have, as you could potentially add them in the future, or use them as an alternative if your current niche is not turning out successfully. As always, expand your knowledge as much as possible, so that you can better determine the best possible outcomes for your business.

What products will you sell?

From there, you will need to determine what products you would like to sell. Consider using keyword tools to help you gather research into how often people search for certain products, and use this to determine what are the best products to sell.

Make sure to identify what fees are associated with each product. Weight, size and storage requirements will vary depending on your product, so look for products with lower fees to minimize your expenses.

Do your best to keep away from products that are used by popular brand names and are well-established in the markets. These are infinitely harder to compete with.

Product Sourcing

Once you've determined the core products that your niche will center around, you will need to find out where your products will be sourced from. You should be looking for supplies with high quality products available for you to sell.

If you intend to sell a product that is produced locally, you could head to your local manufacturer and I'm positive they will be welcoming to your efforts.Alternatively, you could still take the route of using an overseas supplier, which is also beneficial as it tends to bring potential for higher profit margins for your business.It would be to your own benefit to test the products that you are planning on selling, should you find yourself sourcing from an overseas supplier. Try to get your hands on some samples so that you can ensure you will be providing high quality items to your future clients.

Your next step will be to ship the goods to an Amazon Fulfillment Center. Amazon will provide you with specifications and instructions when going through this process. Be sure to keep shipping costs in mind, as these can derail your business if you fail to keep track of them.

Creating your brand

You now have products ready to be sold, however, you're still going to need a brand. Your brand will tell your clients who you are. Make sure to research if your brand name has already been used or not, as well as whether there is an available domain. Your domain name is your website's name, and this will be where clients are able to find you.

Even though you gain more brand will gain more credibility through Amazon, it is still important for you to place high value on its creation. This will define your business for as long as it exists, and so you need to make sure it starts off on the right foot. Remember the main facets of a brand are its name, tagline, logo and the brand story.This will also include your products and how you choose to display them.

Create your product pages, making sure your product details are accurate and detailed, while product photos are professional that emphasize and show off your products. Take a look around to see how other brands market their own products, using this to guide you in your own marketing.

Make sure the tone of your descriptions are friendly and enticing to potential buyers. 'Sell' the product, but don't let them feel that you are selling it. Use the descriptions to make clients feel like this is something they **must** buy; that they can't live without. Be expressive in your writing. Make sure any paragraphs you have are structured and organized so that they are attractive to the reader. Too much boxed all together will feel a little overwhelming.

The aim of the description is to sell the product, and to silence all doubts a client may have regarding their purchase.

Marketing

Your Amazon FBA business is all set up. Now we have to market it. As it is with dropshipping, advertising is the key component to get your business up and running and bring in sales.

Social media is still your best friend here. Look at enhancing your brand's profile, allowing people to view, like, comment and share as you go along. This ensures that you begin to build a rapport with potential customers.

However, don't rush yourself into exploring several channels for marketing at once, and try to invest time in all of them simultaneously. Instead, select a few channels or platforms to begin with, and once you feel you are gaining a return, you can move onto something else.

Here, there is a benefit to influencers, as you can use them to market your product for you. Offer them free products in return for reviewing and marketing your products, and you may see your sales gain a significant boost.

On top of this, consider adding platforms on your website and social media for clients to leave reviews of their purchases and service, as great reviews can give you a massive reputation boost for future customers. Drive your current and potential customers to sign up for email subscriptions. Use your website to find interesting, but not overwhelming ways of enticing your clients to sign up for a subscription. (Smale, 2019)

A Few Extra Tips

Make it a consistent goal to improve your Best Sellers Rank (BSR). The term being fairly self-explanatory, having a business with consistent BSR growth will show clients that your business has tremendous potential to succeed, and that you are reliable in the quality that you offer.

Stay ahead of the trends, and provide more offers to your clients whenever possible. Continue to include products that will compliment the ones that you already have yet provide more variety in selection.

You could also continue to increase your revenues by becoming an affiliate with

Amazon. However, we'll discuss affiliate marketing in detail a little later.

With Amazon's extensive brand and tools available to you, there is a world of endless possibilities that await you, should you choose Amazon FBA to further your venture.

Chapter 4: Affiliate Marketing

Now, as previously mentioned, we'll move onto affiliate marketing. If you've heard of affiliate marketing before, I imagine you're thinking it may be complicated and not worth the effort. However, if you've done any prior research on passive income previously, you'd know that affiliate marketing is considered one of the go-to opportunities when it comes to passive income.

So what is affiliate marketing?

Affiliate marketing is the process with which you can earn commission by promoting another company or person's products. Although revenue is earned through different pay schemes, the general idea is that you will earn an income for each sale you make on the product that you have successfully marketed. This adds legitimacy to the term "Get Paid as you Sleep," as you will earn revenue every time someone uses your affiliate code, or clicks on the link that you have provided. The potential income you receive can vary wildly, from a few bucks here to thousands and possibly even millions. It is all about the manner in which you promote, the traffic you receive, and how you use the skills you have acquired to persuade your clients to purchase something.

Unlike dropshipping and Amazon FBA, you are not in any directly involved with the products, their purchasing or their shipping. You are solely responsible for the marketing of that product. However, this does not mean you should become an affiliate for just about anything. You are not just representing a product, as the product is also representing you and your credibility with clients. The emphasis here is still to ensure that you are associated with high quality products that will help in establishing trust and reliability with your clients.

Even if you've never traveled, I am sure that you've heard of TripAdvisor before. TripAdvisor is a website designed to provide helpful hints, tips and suggestions on places such as hotels and restaurants in various locations around the globe. And guess what? TripAdvisor is an affiliate! You would never have even guessed it, yet the site receives around 116 million visitors every month, earning income from travel companies, hotels as well as other travel sites. They are perhaps one of the largest success stories of affiliate marketing.

Again, not everyone is guaranteed this side of success. However, it could help to merely supplement your salary and ensure that you will live comfortably, or buy that car that you've always wanted. Remember that we are not trying to engage in get rich quick schemes. We are aiming to create an environment where we can live our lives with purpose, while pursuing our dreams. At the end of the tunnel, the reward is very much worth the risk, if you have played the right cards.

Creating an Affiliate Marketing Scheme

As with all of the forms of passive income we have looked at so far, you will need to find a niche for which you can become an affiliate. You might be asking, "If it's just advertising, why do I have to find a niche?" Well, for one, it provides your website with a more organization and structure, and allows you to attract a market, rather than going for the general public. When people are searching for a certain product or service, you will want them to be attracted to your website, and from there to go on and purchase something. This is the advantage of a niche market. Remember the example of TripAdvisor? They provide various options and suggestions for aspiring travelers to consider when planning their holiday. That is their niche.

In this case, it is wise to also consider whether there is space for another affiliate marketer within your chosen niche. Just like you would tend to avoid entering a product market that competes with the largest brands, it is preferable to avoid entering a bloated affiliate market. Are you able to provide competition and make a return? If the answer is yes, then by all means, go for it! Consider a niche that has a broad space for affiliates, so that your options for revenue remain as expansive as possible.

Research is key

From there, it is time to start researching affiliate programs, in order to decipher the products that you will aim to promote. Don't be afraid of taking your time in making the right choice, as it will be well worth your while in the end!

Look for programs that have higher returns and are more profitable. Keep in mind that physical products usually generate lower commission rates than informative products and services. However, each one of these can most certainly be just as profitable as the other. You have to consider what is right for you.

As an example, if you find yourself promoting physical products, signing up with Amazon's affiliate program gives you a 24-hour commission bonus. What this means, is that any product sold in the 24 hours after a customer clicks your link will grant you the commission. Others have long programs, from a month to 90 days. It's up to you to determine the right fit.

Create your website

Now it's time for you to build a site. To begin, you will have to purchase a domain. The domain is the address of your website. NameCheap and DreamHost are two options to consider, however there are several more that are available. Look for an option to purchase that meets your financial constraints.

Once you have done that, it is now time to purchase and setup a host. The host is the place where you will find your site. It is where the entirety of your site resides. Both hosting and domain purchases are fairly affordable, so don't be afraid to move forward, as it neither will be too costly, provided you find the right option for you. Although you will have to take into consideration your financial ability, avoid going for the cheapest option for web hosts. Look for reliable, quality hosting platforms such as BlueHost or HostGator.

Once you've established a host, you're going to need a Content Management System. CMS, for short. CMS is software provided to you, allowing you to create and manage a website without any need for technical, in-depth knowledge of web development or design. This streamlines the process of creating a website, as you don't have to learn any sort of programming in order to start building your website.

If you're a beginner to building a website using CMS, consider using WordPress as it is user friendly and fairly straightforward. However, the choice is yours if you'd prefer another platform. Try to keep it simple in your creation, as you might find yourself overcomplicating things if you're trying to add too much visual appeal. A simple theme will do.

Website Content

The next step is to create content for your site. Your content should remain relevant to your niche, while remaining intriguing and engaging with your target audience. Your content should be interesting enough to retain your existing audience, while still bringing in new members. Product reviews can be useful to provide your clients with assistance in determining what are the best products for them to consider. You could be providing comparison quotes, as a way of seeing how one product matches up against the other. Think of times when you were unsure what smartphone to purchase. You probably looked online to compare the devices to see which would be the best for you.

Another alternative is blog posting. Blogs ensure that you have a consistent structure to building content on your site.Alongside all of this, consider dishing out free informational products, such as an email subscription series, or an ebook. This can help to generate more interest in any product you are trying to sell.

Building a follower base

Once this is complete, it is now time for you to build your audience. If your content is of the highest level, you will eventually start bringing traffic through to your site consistently.

Here, follow the same methods that you would always use. Turn to social media. Another potential option is to use someone else's audience to build your own. Consider writing content for a few blogs whose traffic is fairly high. Remember to make sure that these blogs are also relevant to your niche. You will garner less attraction if you decide to engage with a completely different market, and that is not healthy for your prospects.

If you have the financial capability, you may want to consider investing in paid advertising.

Advertising in the right places can definitely improve the traffic to your site. You may also consider the prospect of SEO. Search Engine Optimization(SEO) is the process of attempting to boost your search engine ranking. What does this mean? Well, if you find yourself looking for a website to purchase video games online, you will naturally use a search engine. When you do, I am positive that you do not sift through the hundreds of pages that are dished out to you. Instead you probably look at the links found on the first page. The aim of SEO is to be on that first page. Think about that for a second. Imagine that when people are searching for something related to your niche, your website is the first to show up. This could potentially drive your traffic through the roof!

Consider hiring an SEO professional, or taking the time to learn it yourself, using their techniques and principles in order to build your audience. (Ogle, 2019)

Promoting Your Offers

Now that you have built up an audience, it is time to kickstart your promotions! You have already shown people that the content you provide is interesting and relevant to them. Now they are willing to listen to you. Promoting content can be done in a variety of ways, depending on you and your site.

One of these techniques is "In-text links." While your audience is reading your content, they may come across links to certain products or services. Should they decide to click on the link and purchase that product or service, you will make a commission on the sale. In-text links are a subtle but effective way of promoting offers, as they are structured around your content, and ensure that your audience is not being bombarded with a sales pitch, which they may not appreciate.

Another option, mentioned previously, are product reviews. Once your audience is willing to listen to and trust you, they will be more accepting and reliant on your opinion. The idea here is not just to point out all of the positives and ignore the negatives. You will need to be honest about your own experience of the product and your thoughts of it in general. It would be better appreciated if you are specific, and describe your offer and product in great detail. From there, you can provide your affiliate link to the offer, and should it be purchased, you've made a sale!

Affiliate Marketing is mostly about quality and strategy. The strategy you have, to develop quality content, and from there, market your affiliate products. You'll notice that the very last thing mentioned was making a sale. That's because we started with the planning and development, and from there looked to develop the quality needed to attract people. Then it was about promoting our affiliate products effectively. Once that happened, it would now be possible to make a sale. You will find that most of these steps will be repeated consistently throughout your venture as an affiliate marketer. However, the sale should be the furthest thing from your mind. Let it happen naturally, rather than trying to force a sale.

If you follow the steps, and you have researched the markets in-depth, I have no doubt that great success can be achieved on your road to true prosperity.

Chapter 5: Blogging

Unlike many of other passive income sources listed in this book, blogging is one of those that most people have been well aware of, but never quite learned too much about it.

What is a Blog?

Simply put, a blog is a sort of online diary. These blogs can be used for the individual, or engaging with others as a more public use. These blogs can include pictures, videos or just plain old-fashioned text.

Started in 1994, blogs have gone from strength to strength in a variety of different categories; from networking, to collective hobby interests to advertising and promotion. Unlike many other aspects of the Internet, instead of being upstaged by other platforms, blogging has diversified its uses. Out of approximately 2 billion websites that exist on the Internet, hundreds of millions of them are blogs. One blogging platform can have around 400 million blogs and users alone, showing their incredible growth and popularity.

As a blogger, you will have the freedom of being able to work whenever and wherever you want, while making money from it. In essence, blogging is the passion, and money can be an added benefit. Blogging gives us the ability to do what we love, while earning money for it. That's what we want, right? Of course!

However, how can this be used to earn any income? Well, that is entirely dependent on you. As mentioned earlier, including affiliate offers within your blogs can help you to earn an income while performing a hobby and sharing your interest.

An alternative to this, would be to sell advertising on your site. This will usually require you to have a very large stream of traffic to have any sort of meaningful return. Usually, I would suggest that this act as a supplement to another source of passive income.

Generally, with blogging, the idea will be to combine with other forms of passive income to create the revenue. A first example would be dropshipping. You could offer products relevant to your blog for others to consider for purchase. So if you have a blog centered around makeup, you could offer cosmetics for others to use as a way of generating income.

Two other alternatives, which we'll discuss in greater detail later in this book, are selling e-books or online courses. This may mean that your initial involvement may be substantially increased, but the rewards for it are increasingly justified, especially since there are zero costs involved in the creation of these products.

The ideas you use will depend on the type of blog you want to create, and the skills you possess that will benefit your business.

Your Own Blog Site

So you've decided to start your own blog. Well, I'm going to sound like a stuck record at this point, but again, you have to start by choosing a niche. However, this time, things are a little different. Whereas in previous chapters, you would choose a niche based on your personal interest and its profitability; this time, you would choose a niche solely based on your personal knowledge and interests, where there is generally a common interest.

There are over 8 billion people in the world today. Somehow choosing a niche that nobody is interested in is most certainly going to be a hard task for anyone at this point. If you fancy a blog based on the theory that the world is flat, I am sure that you will find an audience looking to engage in this thoughtful endeavor with you. Likewise, if you want to write up a blog detailing your belief that aliens live on Mars, you could probably find support for that too!

Granted, most of us wouldn't be so outlandish, and so the niche you fill yourself into would generally be one where there is a large collective interest. What matters is how you manage to reach that audience. However, we'll reach that point a little later. To begin, you have to actually create a blog.

What will you need to begin your first blog? A blogging platform, of course. Choosing the right blogging platform is essential to your needs and skills. To start, you need to consider the type of blog you would like to have.

Is it going to be predominantly text-based, or will it be incredibly picture heavy? For example, if you wanted something text-based, you could use WordPress, which is fairly popular and easy to use, however if you needed a platform that would accommodate a blog that is focused around images, then you would consider Tumblr. If you were looking for something that was more of a mixture, then you could consider Medium.

How much experience do you have when it comes to blogging? Can you handle a platform with severely advanced customization, or do you need something a little more beginner friendly?

Does the blogging platform have any restrictions when it comes to monetization. This is integral, as you don't want to start up a blog on one platform, only to realize that your suggested revenue stream is against their policies.

Finally, what are your financial constraints? Some blogging platforms will require you to have a subscription, while others like WordPress are completely free, however you will have to front the cost for the purchase of a domain.

These are all questions that you will need to ask yourself before you decide to move forward, to avoid any potential hiccups along the way.

As always with having your own website, you need to purchase a domain and a web host to allow the site to run online. Once again, find the options that are cost effective for you, while maintaining quality.

Building Your Blog

The next step is to plan the details of your blog.

What is the aim of your blog, and how much time are you willing to donate to blogging? The aim is something you probably already know, given you have determined your niche as well, but on top of that, you need to consider the amount of time that you have. Granted, you may have a full-time job, kids, or many other factors that keep you occupied. Blogging has to work around this, to ensure that you are still organized in your daily life, and won't leave this behind when you feel notably overwhelmed.

What feelings do you want to invoke in your audience? This helps to determine the tone and setting of your blog. It will ensure that you are finding and writing the right material centered around the aim that you wish to create.

And lastly, how will you manage to attract your audience into using any

one of your chosen revenue streams? Look at how you will plan to market these streams, and what steps to take to persuade your audience into a purchase. This should be the last thing to consider, as it will be based around the content you wish to create, and so ensuring quality content should be your foremost priority.

Now you have a plan, and it is time to design your blog on your chosen platform. It's okay to be tempted to go nuts on the creation, however you'd do well to keep it simple to start. As your experience grows, and you have an idea of using design as a focused point of attraction, you can modify however you see fit. For now, it just needs to be neat and well presented. That, in itself, is interesting to a potential audience. A cluttered blog will merely drive them away. Look at it from the perspective of the audience that you aim to attract and move from there.

Once this is done, it's time to get writing! This part is entirely of your own doing.

Promotion is integral

Now that you have a blog up and running with a few posts, it's time to promote your blog. At this point, I'm sure you know the basics of promoting a few forms of passive income. If your blog contains images, consider using Pinterest and Instagram to promote snippets of your blog, so that others will be keen to see more. As we mentioned with affiliate marketing, consider using other more popular blogs to build up and develop your audience. Use email marketing as a way to notify your current readers of upcoming posts, to ensure they continue coming back for more.

Monetization

Now you need to monetize your blog. As I said earlier, there are several ways you can go about this. If your blog has potential for products that are relevant to your niche, consider dropshipping or affiliate marketing.

As your blog continues to grow in popularity, you may begin to receive offers from advertisers, looking for their own opportunities. You could choose to sell them advertising space directly, or an alternative could be to use Google Adsense, streamlining the process and removing the direct content. We'll learn more about Google Adsense in an upcoming chapter.

The benefits of a blog is that you can combine several aspects of passive income together, although I wouldn't suggest doing that, as you don't want your blog to come across as a money making scheme. Bar the case of ad space, your income form should supplement and be relevant to your content and vice versa, so that there is a direct association between the two.

With the right attitude, blogging could be one of the most engaging and pleasurable ventures that you could potentially immerse yourself in.

Chapter 6: Kindle Publishing

If you find that you have a talent for writing, or you already spend time writing as a hobby, then Kindle Direct Publishing (KDP) may be a fantastic option for you. Usually, if you would like to publish a book you've written, there are two ways to go about it. Having it published by a publishing house, which arouses the possibility of being rejected, or self-publishing, where you take on the decision to publish the book yourself. Given Amazon holds onto a vast majority of the eBook market, they would be the logical choice to use in the case of self-publishing.

Amazon Kindle Direct Publishing allows authors to independently publish their own works on the Kindle store platform (Written Word Media, 2019). On top of being the leaders of the eBook world, they have introduced a paperback option, which provides an alternative to those who prefer the look and feel of a book between their fingers.

Usually, in these cases, the traditional market trumps the newer market in all aspects but one: convenience. However, with self-publishing, that is not entirely true. The self-publishing market has several benefits over the traditional market, especially and most importantly in terms of time. The time it takes to secure a publishing deal can vary from months to years. In today's world, that would be insanity, given you could simply sign up on Amazon and have your book published the very same day, and payment arriving in a few months.

Crucially, the self-publishing market allows you to reach the entire global market, freeing you up for even greater potential for income along the way. Kindle is a fantastic platform for indie authors to finally get their works out there, and start earning an income on them. In terms of royalties, Amazon offers about 60% more than the average publishing house, ensuring your earning potential is much greater if you manage to achieve a decent amount of sales. This really is a fantastic market for anyone who sees writing as a hobby, as the work involved aside from the writing is minimal, and allows you to focus your passion into a reliable income.

Where to Begin

Although you may be inclined to think that once you have written your book, you can pass it off for Amazon, and that will be that; that is not the case. There are several things you need to consider once your book is complete.

Designing your book

So let's look at the following scenario...You have a book. You have the title, the words, the description. What now? Well, consider all the eBooks you've come across, as well as the books you have and see in stores everywhere.

Let's begin with the title. Your title should build up a sense of curiosity in a potential reader's mind. It should intrigue and capture them; make them want to know more. Here is where your cover design complements your title. You need a cover design that is bold and interesting, while complementing your title. We've all seen that some of the best books have the most amazing cover designs. The fact of the matter is, there really isn't much option of reading the first 100 pages to determine whether this is something interesting, so you have to capture their visual senses with the design, and their emotional senses with the title.

A word of warning to the wise. Unless you've professionally designed a cover before, don't do it. This is where quality needs to be at its highest, and you may need to be prepared to spend a bit of money to make more money. There are plenty of publishing companies and individuals that would be happy to help here, for a price. If you're on a really tight budget, you could consider Fiverr, however make sure the designer's samples are of a reasonable quality.

The next step to consider is what the inside of your book looks like. Is it written in a font that is pleasing on the eye? Is it structured and organized and easy to read? You could have answered yes to all of these questions, but I would still suggest that you take the time to hire a professional editor or editing software. With the editing software, you can paste in your content and it will change the formatting before passing it back to you. I personally prefer the human option, as an editor can benefit you in using formatting that can be emotive and correspondent with your writing tone and style. Something an artificial intelligence is not capable of. Once this is done, be sure to proofread it using Kindle, to ensure there aren't any further issues that need to be fixed.

Now, I would be remiss if I failed to mention book description. It is a common misconception that the entire purpose of the description is merely to provide a summary of what the book is about. It is irrelevant whether the book is fiction or nonfiction. The purpose of your description, along with your title and cover design, is to make the reader believe they **need** to read your book. They need to believe it is a necessity before they can continue on with their lives.

In the case of nonfiction, the description should include a little detail on the purpose of the book, the benefit to reading the book, using emotive adjectives to convey emotions into the reader, as well as a call to action. A call to action gives the suggestion to readers that they should buy your book. Sounds rather basic, but altogether this actually works.

In the case of fiction, you'd want to create a scenario for your reader. Remember that you're trying to be mysterious about the contents of your book. By the end of your description, the reader should have more questions than answers. Don't make the mistake of mixing curiosity with confusion. Your book description should still be understandable and intriguing, but must have the reader desperately wanting to know what happens next. That desperation could lead them to buy your book.

You could say that all of this is the first step in the marketing of your book. It's your presentation, so to speak.

Publishing

Now that you have your book, it's time to have it published. However, you have two options to consider. The first is Kindle Direct Publishing. The second is KDP Select. Both of these options are the same in almost all regards except one. KDP Select requires you to be entirely exclusive. What this means is that your eBook cannot be sold anywhere else. Given that we know that Amazon controls most of the eBook market, this isn't too much of a loss. However, it's up to you and what options you would like to have available to you.

Make sure you can place your book in the correct categories, so that if someone is searching related to your book, they could potentially stumble on your book. Look for other books within the category that match up with some of the aspects of your book.

From there, determine your price for it, and publish! Really? It's not that simple? Yes, it is! Publish the book!

Moving Even Further

If this is your first book, chances are you're going to get off to a slow start. Once the first book is published, I would suggest that you begin to put preparations in place to promote any potential titles in the future.

One of the features you can introduce is a review system. Consider starting up a blog or providing a social media link, where they can leave their reviews based on the book they've read. Encourage readers to leave their honest opinions, providing something to make it worth their while, such as a discount on your next book or a free printed version. You can also use your blog or social media account to inform your readers of any future projects you have in mind and once they have been completed. Consider finding out what your readers like to read about. Chances are that these will be closely related to what you have written, anyway.

Once you are ready to publish your next book, consider handing out a few free copies of the book to your readers before release, so that they have time to review it beforehand. This will give your book more credibility once it hits the virtual shelf, and can aid in bringing more customers to your works. Send out emails to your loyal readers a week before launch, so that they are ready to purchase it upon release.

If you'd like to focus a bit on the monetary side of things, then I would consider shifting your price up once a week after release. Usually this is because you would release your book at a lower rate than usual, but raise it from there. Notify your readers that you will be changing the price, as this gives them an incentive to rush to buy the book. Nobody likes missing out on a great deal!

Although these are some of the things you can do to help in boosting your potential sales, the main aspect of this passive income is always going to be your book. If your book resonates with its readers and proves a legitimate success, you're more likely to retain those readers and they may even pass on recommendations to their friends and family. As more people read your book, more people will be interested in your work, and more people will recommend you. This can be quite fulfilling, as you are doing something that you absolutely enjoy, and others are loving it just as much!

Chapter 7: Social Media Marketing

Ah. Social Media. In the current age, I don't see any of us living without it. Useful in so many ways, from keeping in contact with long-lost family and friends to developing and reaching out to the audience of your business. As you've seen so far, social media will play a big role in any business venture you turn to, as it is the one thing that is most easily accessible to everyone.

So what is social media marketing?

It's fairly self-explanatory. It is the process of using various social media platforms to build and engage with an audience in order to develop your brand or drive traffic to a website. So how can you build a passive income out of this? Well, as mentioned previously, you could use it to drive sales in one of your other forms of income. However, since we are looking at using it as a form of passive income, one thing to consider is starting your own marketing agency.

Like many forms of passive income, a social media marketing agency gives you the freedom of being able to work anywhere, anytime, while giving you a platform into a business with tremendous earning potential. As an agency, you will be there to help other brands grow their business and promote brand loyalty. You will be responsible for engaging with their customers as well as the advertising that is needed. Once you gain reasonable success, you can then begin to take on new clients and take your own brand to greater heights.

How Do I Start My Own Brand?

Stepping into the social media marketing world, is stepping into a vastly expanding industry, so you must be prepared to put in a decent amount of work and stake your claim as a more persuasive choice than other marketers in the field. First, we need to build up your business.

Have a business plan

To begin, you need to develop your business plan. You may need to spend some time investing in yourself, as if you haven't done any kind of social media marketing before, you don't really want to head into this flying blind. Extensive research will be needed. Consider doing a few free courses, as well as few paid ones as well. Once you feel you have gathered as much knowledge as you possibly can about the industry, it is time to step in.

Consider building a portfolio of services that you would like to offer your future customers.

This will provide other brands with clarity on the strategies you will use in the services and solutions that you plan to offer. Will you be able to offer analytics or content marketing, or both? Try to find offers that your clients would not find at other social media agencies, in order to set yourself apart.

Professional Links

Next, businesses will need a way to find you. So, you will need to set up a website. As we've gone through this book, I'm sure you've become aware of the processes involved in building a website. Your website should contain all the details on the services you provide, their prices, and contact information. Consider adding details on why you would be a superior choice to any other agency.

Once your website is complete, you need to set up your own agency's social media accounts. It is vital that you have your own presence on social media, is clients would become a bit skeptical to your expertise, if they find that you are not active in that field. Social media will also be the location that you will use to begin marketing your services. Your posts and content on social media will provide a demonstration of skills that you have learned. Use the tools that various social media providers offer to generate wide reaching engagement and increase the number of people you can potentially reach.

Make sure that you provide links to both your website and your social media accounts from each, so that clients can find all of your information easily.

Something you may want to consider, is to start up a blog on your website. You can use these blogs to further demonstrate your understanding and skills in the field. Creating how-to articles, trend coverage and tips posted on your blog will show others that your knowledge is extensive, and would make them more comfortable with considering you as a suitable hiring choice. As a newcomer in the market, your activity on social media platforms as well as the content on your blog will add some credibility to your agency.

Once you have all the basics in place, you will need to find clients who are willing to work with you. Don't think of the big companies just yet. They will most definitely not consider hiring someone without a proven track record. To begin, you need to approach the smaller companies in the hope that you will pick up a few clients. Cold mailing is one of the strategies you can use to pitch yourself to potential clients. Cold mail is reaching out to someone directly without any form of prior contact. Usually, this is used to describe emails that have been sent, but in this case I would suggest using LinkedIn. LinkedIn is a professional social network, designed to help people make business connections and share their expertise, experience and potential find employment. You can message potential clients here describing the services that you provide and why they should hire you.

Consider adding a promotional aspect into your message. For example, should they hire you, they will pay a reduced fee for a short time period, or alternatively, offer a free trial to build confidence in your service.

Always make sure that you are keeping up with the latest trends in social media marketing. You should be keeping an eye on your rivals to make sure that you are always one step ahead, using the latest features and tools that have been introduced on each platform. Even falling slightly behind in the industry can mean you suffer a big loss as competition until the emergence of the next trend you can jump on.

For your social media marketing agency to be successful, the most important thing you need is results. Results will in turn bring more clients. More clients will in turn bring more revenue. However, your main focus should be the quality that you display. Clients will not be impressed if you fail to deliver the services you offered. Even if you have to start with just a single client, prioritize quality over quantity, and the rest will come with it.

A Few Tips Of Note

Once you've developed your social media marketing agency, picked up a few clients and achieved reasonable success, you're going to want to maintain any potential growth. Leaving your agency to stagnate will mean it will fall behind other companies and lose potential clients as time wades on, so you need to be organized and consistent in your approach.

Once you've picked up a few clients and have been fairly successful with them, consider adding a review aspect to your website, linking them with the reviews in order to boost your credibility for the future.

Be open to changing your strategy from time to time. Sometimes, a single strategy will not work in all given scenarios, and you may need to be more flexible to meet your client's and their customers' needs. Always be prepared to analyze and understand how you can position yourself to deliver exceptional quality in every scenario.

Always research your audience. Making assumptions about what you believe your audience will appreciate can be a dangerous game. Make sure that you use all of the tools available to you to find out as much as possible about your audience demographics on each social network.

Using this knowledge, make engagement a priority. The level of engagement you have determines how your audience perceives you and their willingness to interact. You want your audience to feel like they play an active part of the company in your interaction with them. Make sure to strike the right balance with them. You don't want to add too much personality that it takes from the promotional. However, you don't want to be too promotional as this will drive away some of your audience.

Something you should look at for personal development is to set goals for yourself. Set goals that tackle your largest challenges. It could be to add more personality and be more engaging, or be more persuasive in your advertising. This makes sure you are ever improving and developing your expertise, and will benefit your business in the long run. Remember there is always something new that can be learned. You should never stop learning.

There are probably several more useful tips and tricks. However, I believe if this is your chosen field for passive income, you will come across them during the time you spend learning the skills you need, as well as during your time as a social media marketer.

For now, you have all the necessary steps to build your way into the industry and gain the income you desire. From there, the potential of your business is only limited by how far you are willing to take it.

Will you reach for the sky? Or will you reach for the stars? The choice is yours.

Chapter 8: Rental Income

The housing market is probably one of the most enormous markets in the world. Why? We all need somewhere to stay, or we need a premises to act as the base of our business operations. Part of this market is the rental market. When most people are unable or unwilling to purchase a property, they may choose to rent instead. While selling a property results in the seller receiving a bulk payment at the value of the property, rentals provide you with a fixed monthly income at a fee you set for your property for a duration of time.

Renting gives you the opportunity to earn enough income to cover the costs of that property that you have to fill, and provide you with extra as well. Of course, there are certain risks involved. You could end up with a destructive tenant, or a non-paying tenant.

However, one could say that no form of passive income is without its risks, and this is no different. You will have to do the right amount of research into your potential customers before renting out the property.

While the housing market is fairly straightforward, there are a few things to consider to make sure you can get the most out of your business, with reduced risk. If you have another property where you do not live, or an outbuilding attached to your home that is not in use, then a rental income might be the right way forward for you.

Renting Out Your Property

You need to consider your own property first when planning a rental. What type of property is it? Are your tenants going to be using it for residential purposes or business purposes. You will have to decide if the property is in sufficient shape to be offered out. If not, you may need to invest a little in repairing anything that is damaged or broken, while making it look attractive as possible. Remember, you want to find tenants who will be happy living in your premises. This will mean they are more likely to be reliable and pay their bills on time.

From there, consider your neighbourhood, the features of your property and its condition as well. This will help you in determining the price of your rental. The general rule is that your rental fee is in the area around 1% of your home's entire value. However, it's important to note that some places may have control over your rental rate. New York, Maryland and Washington all have varying degrees of rent control laws, so you need to do some extensive research on the rental market and its jurisdictions in your area.

Individual vs. Agency

Once your property is in decent shape, and you have an idea of how much you are going to rent it for, you can plan on renting out your property.

There are two ways to go about this. You could choose to hire an agency who will take care of the business for you, or you could choose to do it yourself. There isn't too much harm in doing it yourself, provided you actually know what you are doing.

There are benefits to both, and the rental agency offers you the benefit of having a tried-and-tested procedure when it comes to renting out properties to tenants. They will streamline the process for you, and handle all the paperwork and communication from the tenant, relaying it back to you. You generally don't have much, if anything to do with the process. The downside being that agents can charge a hefty fee for their services - generally 10% of the rental amount.

On the other hand, you could research the processes and follow them yourself. However, some tenants may have a belief that it's easier to take advantage of individual home owners instead of those who went through an agency. Should any issues occur, you may find yourself struggling with the procedures to follow. In the case of an agency, they will know the direct route to take, and follow it to the tee.

Warning signs to be aware of

However in this case, let's just assume you want to rent your property out independently. You will need to learn how to vet your potential tenants. This is arguably one of the most important aspects of renting. You need to inspect a prospective tenant's past behavior in the form of a credit profile as well as their tenant profile to determine that they have been consistent, and that there are no red flags to consider. Past behavior is usually an indicator of future behavior, so it's best to avoid all clients who have any hiccups on their profiles.

There are a few suspicious behaviors that you will need to be aware of going in. For example, a tenant who asks to enter an agreement in an alternative family member's name, outside of the person responsible for the property, is a sufficient enough risk to consider moving on and finding an alternative tenant.

Another red flag would be a potential tenant who tries to negotiate on the initial sum to be paid. If a tenant asks to pay the initial fee in parts, this may indicate a lack of affordability and will paint a negative picture of their future actions.

Make sure to evaluate your pet policies. Will pets be allowed into your property? If you do allow pets, what pets are suitable to the type of accommodation you are providing.

Finally, evaluate the type of tenants you would like to have. Younger tenants are more likely to cause harm to your property, as well as tenants that have children. Look for tenants who seem responsible and stable in their lives.

Rental Structure

Once you feel that you have a firm grasp on what to look out for, you need to draw up a leasing agreement in advance. This means you are suitably prepared once you have found a tenant that is up to your standards.

Usually, it's possible to find a lease template online; however, it is up to you to ensure that your lease has all the necessary sections and subsections to satisfy your needs.

As an example, some of the more general aspects of the lease to include are:

Tenant Names. This is not just the name of the person responsible, but all tenants on the property.

Length of Tenancy. All rental documents should state how long the term of the lease runs for. You could either have a rental agreement, which runs from month to month and self-renews until terminated, or a fixed-term lease, which usually lasts about a year.

Rental Fee. This should specify the fees to be paid, when it is due, and how it is to be paid. Consider including your payment method as well as any fees related to late payments or check bounces.

Deposits and Additional Fees. Be clear on what you may use the deposit for (damages, overdue bills, cleaning fees) as well as what the tenant is not allowed to use the deposit for (final month's rent). It is also beneficial to include where the deposit is being held, and whether it will accrue any interest.

Damage and Maintenance. Make sure the responsibilities of both the tenant and yourself are well documented in this section so that both yourself and the tenant know where they stand in this regard. Include any restrictions on the tenant altering the property that you would like.

Pets. All restrictions and conditions on pets must be placed here.

Once you are well set and organized, you can begin to advertise your property. Since there is a massive demand for property, you will most definitely receive offers for your property once it is out there. Placing advertisements on social media, property websites, as well as more wholesale websites will all bring prospective tenants straight to you.

As I said in the beginning, this is one of the more straightforward methods of bringing in a passive income, and can be one of the most reliable. It can provide a more stable footing for you to go out and live comfortably.

Chapter 9: Cryptocurrency

The cryptocurrency market has seen massive growth in recent times. You've probably heard bits and pieces about it around the news and maybe from some of your friends.

One of the biggest names in cryptocurrency being Bitcoin, had you invested $100 in Bitcoin in 2011, that investment would have soared to over a million dollars in 2019. In 2017 alone, Bitcoin saw an approximate increase of around 1500%, while another in Ethereum soared to over 10,000%. This just shows the ludicrously dramatic increase that has surged around cryptocurrency. While Bitcoin and a few others have undergone a bit of a rollercoaster ride in recent times, there is no doubt that cryptocurrency is still a great solution to earning additional income for yourself.

If you're still scratching your head to understand what is cryptocurrency, let me explain.

Cryptocurrency is a form of digital currency that conducts financial transactions to make money. This is usually done using cryptography, which is the science of hiding information. Cryptocurrency is entirely independent from government or individual control, which is completely unlike the banks and the money we use today.

Each cryptocurrency works through a ledger; a list of transactions that is shared by everyone, usually in the form of a blockchain. Now, a blockchain is the method of storing a list of entries, which cannot be changed easily once they have been created. This ledger serves as a database of all public transactions. Since the first inception, over 4000 cryptocurrencies have been created. Due to their independence, cryptocurrencies generally have their own interest rates and are not subject to the general rules of inflation or deflation (Blockgeeks, 2019).

Now, although there seems to be a lot of complications around cryptocurrencies, I hope I simplified it enough to give you a general idea of what it is as a market. In reality, it is just a selection of entries in a database that cannot be changed without certain criteria being met. In itself, cryptocurrency has no value.

With a logical mindset, and the right amount of research, you can become a legitimate success in the world of cryptocurrency.

Investing In Cryptocurrency

If you've chosen cryptocurrency to act as your passive income, then there is going to be a steep learning curve you're going to have to master before you start. Extensive research into how the process works, and what steps you need to take to develop your income are of utmost importance. Going in blind will could see you losing all the value you have consistently, so it is important that we minimize risks. Use simulators that work on the real time values to help you get ahead on the learning curve.

The necessary tools

Next, you're going to need to open up a few accounts, with the first being Coinbase. Coinbase will allow you to exchange your cash into cryptocurrency for you to invest with. You could consider using another exchange service, however this is what I find to be the most reliable and secure.

From there, you can set up a purchase for whatever cryptocurrencies you would like to purchase, at the amount you want to invest. Avoid the smaller cryptocurrency companies, as you will be more likely to fall victim to scams on any one of those. Here, it is best to stick with the top providers in the market.

While deciding how much you would like to invest, I would suggest that your initial investment be around 30% of your total investment value. What that means is that you should only invest a small portion of the total amount you have with which to invest, just to get you started, and to ensure you don't have a big loss. The amount of your initial investment must be an amount that you are comfortable with making a loss on, should that occur.

Once you have purchased your chosen currencies, you will need a place to keep them safe. This is called a wallet. You can choose to either have a software wallet or a hardware wallet. Hardware wallets are used in a similar manner to external hard drives. These can be used when you don't plan on accessing currencies anytime soon. On the other hand, software wallets are used when you want to be active in your trading.

Be sure to diversify your portfolio. As you would with regular investments, don't throw all your eggs in one basket. Diversifying your portfolio will help to shield you when currencies become extremely volatile, and help to protect you from overall losses.

Stay clear of mobile wallets, as these tend to be a bit on the suspicious side, and are not as secure as software or hardware wallets.

From there, you're ready to trade. How you choose to trade is purely up to you and your strategy. You could choose to be really aggressive, and go for short term gains, or play the long term game with your investment. The choice is yours.

A Bit Of A Heads Up

Prepare yourself for this type of market, should you choose to invest in it. Cryptos are excessively volatile. A gain five minutes ago could turn into severe losses an hour later. You need to steel yourself to these occurrences, and ensure that you don't act out on rash decision-making and emotions. This is why it is so important to only invest as much as you can afford to lose.

As I've already mentioned, but will mention again; stick with the more reliable cryptocurrency providers. Due to the difficult and independent nature of cryptocurrencies, it can be very easy to get caught up in a scam. You need to be aware what are the signs that something isn't right, and when to move away.

Make sure that you have a reason to enter each trade. Trading impulsively could see you losing at a constant rate. Did you see a pattern? Something that made you consider buying in? Make sure that every investment has a reason behind it.

With that being said, avoid buying simply because the price is low. This is a mistake several newbies make. If they see a drop in price, they will buy in, assuming it's cheaper and will rise in value at some point.

Finally, set goals for yourself. It may sound a bit strange when dealing with such a volatile market, however setting goals will help you establish a medium of what you aim to achieve. Given we're looking at passive income, this could be a target for you to reach each month. However, in this case you will need to be flexible in your goals, to accommodate the volatility.

While you may balk at the amount of risk involved in cryptocurrency, time has proven that there are many ways to minimize that risk and in turn collect huge rewards. In fact, I would say that cryptocurrency has the potential to deal out the largest profits. However, as with all investments, big rewards require big risks. That doesn't mean you can't play it safe. Evaluate what type of trader you want to be and what are the best platforms for you to exercise your strategy and achieve your goals. Remember, the most successful investors will always remain calm in the face of adversity, as they know that another opportunity will always present itself. Emotional traders will always be losing trades, so learn to trade objectively instead, and in time you will reap the benefits of your consistency.

Chapter 10: Google Adsense

If you think about, advertisements have been around for as long as one can remember. They have been the number one way for businesses to promote themselves and their product. As time has continued, ads have remained, but only the medium has changed. Now you could probably find ads in just about every place imaginable, especially in the online market. Just about every website has a few ads here and there, and only a select few claim to be completely ad-free. This could mean that we tons of random ads on varying sites that hold no relevance. That is where Google Adsense comes into play.

Now this is something I mentioned a little earlier when discussing ways of creating income from a blogging site. Google Adsense displays ads on your website that are relatable to the content that you have, as well as based on previous user searches. Once users start clicking those ads, you will receive payment as Adsense works on a system of cost-per-click and shared revenue. What this means is that you will want as many users as possible to click on those ads.

From these clicks you will generally receive a commission cut ranging from anywhere between 20 cents to a couple dollars. Remember, this is earned at a cost per click, so generating a high rate of clicks could grant you a substantial increase in revenue.

It is estimated that around 10 million websites are now using Google Adsense. They provide security and transparency for both the advertisers and publishers. Google makes sure that both sides have a clear understanding of the whole process and everything can be tracked.

On top of this, Adsense is capable of running a variety of formats for its ads. You can run your ads in text, image, video and several others as well. This gives freedom of experimentation to better suit your website.

Google Adsense will also give you the option to block ads that rival your content. This is a handy feature when you find that the ads you are promoting are taking sales away from you and handing it to your competitors.

Using Google Adsense To Make You Money

So now that we've established that Google Adsense can be a source of income, it's time to determine how you can go about doing it. This doesn't involve throwing ads on your website, sitting back and the money will miraculously roll in. You need to invest your time into making it profitable so that you can generate a return.

For starters, you're going to need a website or a blog. As we looked at previously, you're going to need to focus on a niche that you can center these ads around.

When applying for a Google Adsense account, there is going to be a few criteria that you have to consider:

Ensure you own the Domain. Part of the process of your application will require you to verify ownership of your domain. If you can't verify that you own the domain, then Google will reject your application.

Quality Content. We looked at this throughout this book, so I imagine it is no surprise that to be considered, you need to have quality content. This also does not mean you can develop high quality content, and tail off once you pick up some ads. Google will remove your account if they deem your content to not be up to scratch. This is why it is important to consider a passion as your source for a niche. You will be inspired and driven to deliver something interesting and meaningful if you care about it.

The Age of your site. This one is fairly new from Google. You will now be required to own your site and post content for at least six months before you apply for Adsense.

Google Policies and standards. Make sure that your website adheres to all the policies that Google sets forth, as well as their standards and restrictions on certain content.

While this seems like a lot to consider, it is only because Google wants to provide the best content with remuneration and ensure that everything is moderately regulated.

Optimizing The Ad Experience

Once you've passed Google's criteria, you're going to need to make sure that your ads are positioned optimally to generate more clicks. This will center around how you display ads alongside your content. Make sure that they compliment each other; your content will still take preference, but the ads should still stand out.

Consider setting up your ads alongside a Call to Action (CTA). A CTA is a technique that instructs users to perform a particular action on your site. Since CTAs are designed to draw attention to themselves, placing ads around them could potentially draw attention to the ads as well.

Now we get to what I would consider a bit of a hiccup. Adblock tools. As we find ads in more places around the internet, more users are turning to adblock to restrict ads from appearing, so they can focus solely on content. Unfortunately, there isn't much way around this. All you could do is simply ask them in a polite manner, to turn their adblock off. A study revealed that more people would be willing to turn off their adblock feature if you simply asked them to.

Something else to take into note, is the potential amount of mobile users you may have. Smartphones are everywhere, and you would be making quite an error if you chose not to cater to this market. You will need to adjust your site to become not only more mobile-friendly, but you will have to adjust the ads as well to cater to that audience.

Taking your income further

Ideally, if you feel that Adsense is not enough for you, you could opt to increase your earnings by combining with another form of passive income. Affiliate marketing could be a great supplement to the revenue you generate from Adsense. You could also decide to sell your own products and services as well. At the end of the day, it really is up to you how you choose to run your business. Although each of these chapters focuses on one aspect of passive income, you could combine as many as you would like, as long as it is effective and caters to your lifestyle.

While Google Adsense does seem a bit on the stricter side, they are generally asking for what most online providers ask for these days: consistency, suitability and relevance. Making sure you are up to date with their policies and providing quality content should generally be a norm on any platform you use, and so I'm sure that you will grow accustomed to it in no time.

Google Adsense provides a great opportunity to earn income while focusing your time on other income opportunities. Take the opportunity!

Chapter 11: Online Courses

The constant surges in technology have not only given way to increases in advertising and marketing strategies. They have given way to the potential for learning as well. These days, you could probably learn just about anything you want online. From mathematics to programming to the complexities of a cell. All of it is at the touch of your fingertips.

Likely, in such a market, there is always the opportunity to be seized, and creating online courses is one way you could go about it. Creating your own online courses provides you with the chance to share your expertise with others in a constructive manner. As the industry grows, there are several companies capitalizing on the market, hosting entire websites devoted to a variety of topics for prospective learners to access.

It is estimated that around 33 percent of students have taken online courses, however this does not include those who have chosen to learn later in life. Online courses are not just about professional skills and student-based subjects. It can be about anything that you have a talent for or experience in doing. Online courses can be about anything from cooking to writing, to painting tutorials and maybe even lessons on how to be a decent clown performer. Anything really means anything.

The benefits to online learning can be immense, as a learner has the potential to receive a wide variety of teaching methods, such as video and audio content, in order to grasp the concepts of what they are learning. Whereas before, it's well-known that anyone who did a bit of self-learning usually looked at the old-fashioned textbook. Online courses have reinvigorated learning to make it a much more fun and interesting experience.

Creating Your Own Online Courses

Creating your own course is actually somewhat similar to starting up a blog at the beginning. It's funny how all these different options tend to intertwine. As you would pick a niche for your blog that you have an interest in, you would choose a course topic that you are most passionate about. Your training will come off as dull if you decide to engage with a topic you couldn't care less about. However, you will also need to consider the demand for your course. You'll feel rather frustrated if you're creating all these online courses and there's nobody willing to buy them.

Look for gaps in the competition that match your skill sets and experience, to ensure that you are entering a market that is demanding your knowledge. Try to find something that sets you apart from the other course creators in your field. What makes your courses more interesting and exciting than theirs?

Include course outcomes

A key aspect of course creation is to make sure all your courses have course outcomes. It wouldn't be a good idea to hand a course to a learner, and they have no idea what it is they are supposed to be achieving. Students will most likely want to know how your course is going to help them, and if this isn't provided, they may not want to enrol in your course.

The purpose of the learning outcome is to ensure that learners will have a clear understanding of what they will be able to accomplish once they have completed each section of the course, as well as by the end of the course. It should describe the skills they have learned and the knowledge they have gained from completing this course. This will also lead to fewer cases of unhappiness amongst students and fewer refunds to boot.

Plan your content

Once you have outlined what the course is going to achieve, you need to plan the content of your course. Given that this is a field of your talent and expertise, you may be inclined to push the envelope a little too far on what you include. Therefore, instead of considering what you need to include, consider what you need to leave out. This is where the learning outcomes will play a role for you. Anything that is not directly related to the learning outcomes should be removed altogether.

All this content will then need to be ordered into modules and organized. You will need to group all the similar content, tips and ideas together in each of their respective modules, so that the learning is flowing and progressive.

Your course should follow a natural and logical progression in the learning phase.

Teaching methods

Now that all your material is grouped together and organized into a structured course, you need to determine your method of delivery. You will need to be considerate of who it is that you are targeting with your content. Are they adults or children? Both? Consider the various ways you can deliver your course, so that it remains interesting for all of the potential learners you may have. Your method of deliver can include video, audio, reading and exercises to best enhance the learning experience. Try to strike a balance between all of these methods, to keep your learners engaged throughout the course.

Now comes the interesting part! You need to get on camera! Okay, well maybe you don't **need** to, but it is proven that the best way to deliver learning is through video. If you don't feel like getting on camera, you could use screencasting instead. Screencasting is when you display a recording of your screen for video. This way, you can do a voiceover, along with an on-screen tutorial, while you don't have anyone seeing your face.

If you don't want to include a video tutorial at all then that is fine, but consider that you want to maximize your potential for profits as much as possible, and the most effective online learning method will help see to that. (Edition, 2019)

Selling And Marketing Your Course

The course is now complete, and you are ready to have students take your skills and knowledge on board. In order to do that, you need to decide how you're going to sell your online courses. Three of the more legitimate ways to sell your course is through learning management systems, online course marketplaces or through your very own website.

A learning management system (LMS) is basically like having your own little academy, and will function as your very own brand. On the other hand, an online course marketplace is a platform where anybody is allowed to sell online courses on the same site. These sites usually do not keep track or analyse the courses before sales, so a course can be anything from extremely high quality and informative, to extremely low quality and just plain dreadful. You website is, well; it's your website. This decision is really up to you.

Another crucial decision that will be in your hands is the pricing of your courses. Look at your potential competitors to see what they are charging for a similar product. Now comes the controversial part. Consider pricing yours slightly higher than theirs. Why? Well a lower course price will make customers feel like it is of a lower quality, and that will work against you rather than with you.

Now you're probably ready to sell your product, but you need customers. It's back to the good old marketing strategies for you! Even if your course is completed, how are people going to find out much about it?

One thing to consider is to partner up with an influencer who creates content that is relevant to your own. Reach out to various influencers and find out who is willing to market your products.

Make sure that you are always one step ahead in your marketing strategies. This means planning out the strategies you will undertake as time progresses. As the course creator, and the most knowledgeable on the matter, you will know where it is you will find students for your course. With that in mind, I'm sure you've already pinpointed a few places where you could potential market your course. Social media, once again, will be your friend.

Make sure to persuade any students you do receive to sign up for email notifications, so that you can inform them when you do have another course being rolled out, especially when it all falls under one ongoing subject.

And there you have it. Online courses provide the perfect opportunity to share your wealth of skills with the world, developing and earning a profit while helping others to pick up new skills themselves. Pretty nifty, don't you think?

Chapter 12: AirBnB Business

Traveling is something that we would like to do or that we all love to do. Generally, I imagine every one of us would leap on board the opportunity to travel were we given the chance. However, the sad truth is that for many of us, the costs involved are just too great. From flights, to hotels, to food and drinks, there are so many expenses that we have to consider. However, Airbnbs have come about to help alleviate some of these costs.

Airbnb is an online marketplace where travelers can find hosts to book space in various accommodations around the world. If you're interested in the term, Airbnb comes from air mattress B&B, where B&B stands for bed and breakfast. Airbnbs provide travelers with an incredibly expansive list of options for accommodation, at a much cheaper rate than you would pay to stay at a hotel. This also provides the chance for travelers to "live like a local", enhancing their overall experience.

All that you would do is list your property on the website, and then wait for reservations. Given these are short term rentals, you may be a bit on the fence about whether to opt for a longer term standard rental or an Airbnb. However, short term stays can be beneficial in their own right. You get to enjoy having new guests and meeting new and exciting people every few days. This can provide you with an opportunity to experience and interact with a variety of people from different cultures while presenting your own cultures to them.

You'll also have the option to be flexible in your pricing. Airbnb allows you to change your price listing as often as you'd like, should you wish to. With all this in mind, should you have a property that you have available, that you would like to rent out, consider using Airbnb to provide future travelers with a comfortable home from home.

Setting Up An AirBnB

First things first. Make sure you're acquainted with the laws in your area. There are some places where Airbnb hosting is banned, while in others, it is regulated. Make sure you are extremely knowledgeable about the regulations in your area so that you can avoid any serious troubles later on.

Decide your hosting calendar

You will need to decide how often a year you would like to host. Airbnb allows you to set the dates and months you would like to be available for hosting as well as the maximum or minimum permitted time that a guest is allowed to stay.

Security

Although Airbnb provides their own assurances when it comes to damages, consider taking out insurance on special items in your home that are not covered by Airbnb's guarantee. This will give you peace of mind if any rowdy occupiers end up causing damage to your home. To partially circumvent these kinds of problems, consider the type of traveler you would like to appeal to. Is your property located close to the business district? If so, consider targeting business travelers who have an agenda within the district. Always look to appeal to the market you want.

Knowing and exceeding the competition

Make sure that you know what Airbnbs are around the same area as you as they will likely be your main competition. Research their properties to determine where you can receive an edge in the market to push yourself above them in demand from travelers. Make sure your property is clean and well maintained, so that it can decorated into something extremely appealing to your guests.

Make sure that you have the amenities that are essential to your guest's needs as well as those that deliver a wonderful experience. Try to invest a bit in stylish furniture and artwork to make your property more vibrant and interesting. Guests will always go for the property that is pleasing on the eyes, and so it is integral to maintain just that.

Your Airbnb Profile

Your profile with Airbnb is arguably going to be the most important feature of your business. As customers will not be able to pay a visit to check out your property, they will rely on the information you gave about the listing to determine if it is suitable.

You will need to set up your home type, location, whether they will rent the "Entire place," or will they be a part of a group of shared guests? Make sure you know exactly how many guests your property can accommodate in total. Any form of overbooking can lead to all sorts of problems, and none of them are where you will come out on top.

Next, you will need to set up the actual profile of your property. This is more or less advertising your property to potential tenants.

Make sure you have snapped some professional photos of the different areas of the home to show off on the page. Try to take pictures where a room is cast in light, and looks masterful in presentation. The better the pictures, then more people will be keen to stay on your premises. Show off the different rooms, amenities and other features that are unique to your property.

Potential guests will also be interested in the description that you provide, as this needs to paint a portrait of how exciting and interesting your property is. Try to include a bit of your personality in your description, in order to make your property shine. Avoid writing too much, as this will become a bit exhausting to read. Use short sentences and bullet points so that you are emphasizing your points.

Once you have uploaded pictures and completed your description, make sure to list all the amenities that your property has. I mean **all** of them. There are many features that people will look for, and some are more specific than others. These could be that make or break that determines whether a traveler opts for your property instead of another.

One thing to do to help your guests is offer extra services, such as transport from the airport for an added fee. Given they are in a new location, this might be a welcome addition for those who have just hopped off a plane and can think of nothing better than to have a decent sleep as soon as possible.

Once your guests have arrived, make sure to greet them and provide them with a tour of where they will be staying. Give them a rundown of the area, and suggest some attractions for them to potentially visit. Make sure that your guests feel well-treated, and try to be on hand to provide assistance as much as possible. Do your utmost to make any guests feel at home during your stay. Why? Well, Airbnb includes a review service on their website, which is also a part of your property listing. In a world where there is much uncertainty, having decent reviews can be the difference between a traveler deciding between a competitor and yourself. If you have the better, more consistent reviews, then these clients will be more likely to stay on your property instead. Treat the moment as an experience to learn about someone new. This way, you will be more eager to help them with anything they may need, and they will most definitely be more willing to engage with you.

While Airbnb is not one of those markets with unlimited potential, it provides an ideal option for those looking to gain something of a second salary for several parts of the year, in order to better their financial position.

Chapter 13: Dividend Investments

Let's look at some of the more well-known methods that we see being used all the time. Now, most people see stocks as this terribly toxic monster that they never want to venture anywhere near. Others spot opportunities to make money. Those who are too fearful simply do not spot the chances available to them to grow their money. They fail to spot that there could potentially a agap to increase their earnings, without suffering huge losses. Dividend Investing is one of those opportunities.

Unlike other investments, dividend stocks are stocks that allow you to generate a steady stream of income. The purpose here is to build short term income, while setting up long term wealth. How does this work? Well, the idea is that you would invest in a company that pays out dividends during the course of the year. That could range from every few months to twice a year. Dividends are the monies paid out to shareholders out of a company's profits (My Accounting Course, 2019).

This allows you to create a steady income stream during the course of a year, while your wealth generates over a longer term. As that term increases, so do your potential payouts. Most consumers ideally want shorter term rewards, and dividend stocks provides an opportunity for those to occur.

Although stocks inherently carry risks, with extensive research you can learn how the best traders operate so that you can minimize your own risks and receive constant reward.

Investing In Dividend Stocks

When it comes to stocks, you're going to need to do extensive research into the trade. You need to learn how to read the stocks, spot trends, use the tools and several other factors that will govern your role as a successful stock investor.

Have an investment strategy

Going in, you will need to have a strategy on how you choose to invest. Determine how you're going to generate better long term returns. Given you will still generate dividends over the year, your goal will always be to find the best long term stock options.

What to look for in stocks

Don't buy stocks simply for the sake of dividends is a crucial error that many investors can make when starting out. You may find a company has a high dividend yield, however their stock is falling dramatically. Include the potential taxes in this, and you will simply be at a standstill or begin making losses on your investment. On top of that, it is unwise to simply invest in high-dividend stocks, as these could be a sign of problems within the business or low future growth. This will damage any long term investments you will make.

Payout Ratios

Look for important numbers such as **The Payout Ratio**. The Payout Ratio is the amount of earnings that is paid out to shareholders, expressed as a percentage. There is no ideal payout ratio, however this ratio can help you in determining a few factors about a company. For example, if a company's payout ratio is fairly high, say around 58% or higher, you may find that this is a sign that this company is issuing too many of their earnings to shareholders.

On the opposite side, a company with lower payout ratio may be related to low performance. At the same time, a company with high payout ratios but low performance have seen their earnings fall over time, but the dividends remain the same. Dividends that pay less than 50% with signs that the rest is going back into the business will bring about future growth.

You need to consider a company's overall track record over a number of years in order to assess whether they are a healthy option to invest in. A company with healthy growth and strong payout ratio may be a fantastic opportunity to invest.

Dividend Yield

The next aspect you will need to consider is the dividend yield. This is the return you will receive from your investment in the form of payments. However, there are key indicators you will need to watch out for. For example, if the dividend yield goes up, it could be a result of falling stock. A fairly normal dividend yield should be considered between 2% and 6%.

Consistency

This is one of the most important aspects when looking at dividend stocks. Think of it as the credit record of a stock. You'll want to be looking for companies that have been consistent in raising their dividend payments, or have generally kept these payments the same over a number of years, no less than three.

Picking individual stocks is a tough business, so it's imperative to ensure that you know what you are doing, especially since most of us don't. One thing to consider is that you are trying to secure an income. While there may be others with cash to burn, looking to make high risk manoeuvres in the market, you're trying to protect your money and attain a reasonable safety net.

Look for companies that have high returns on equity, with little to no debt. These are signals that the business is of fairly good standing, and could provide a good cushion should anything problematic occur.

Dividend investing, like most stock trades, is mostly about predicting the future possibilities and standings of a business. Predicting correctly can lead to consistent returns and increased income and stock value, so that you can build an income that you can not only live comfortably on, but at the very end, you can receive value from the stocks you spent years accumulating, which could end up being a nice retirement treat.

You're going to want to **pay attention to the companies that pay these dividends**. It's not just about the finances involved and their credibility. Look at whether it is a company that you want to invest in. Consider the business model as well. The way a company is run can tell you a lot about its future prospects. Consider yourself as part of this company. You're a shareholder, so get to know it!

Learn how to **use dividend yields to tell if a stock is overvalued or undervalued**. This can tell you a bit about the current trajectory of the stock market and its potential trends. Learn a few methods to determine this, so that you can understand the risks that you take when purchasing a stock.

You can **use your dividends to help you recover from your losses**. If you took a big hit in the value of your investments, you may want to use your dividends to reinvest and rebuild over the next period of time. This will help you to ensure longer term stability.

Diversify your stocks. As you would with cryptocurrency, diversifying your stock profile will help to provide a safety blanket should one of your investments fall. Never hedge your bets all on just a few stock options.

Try to invest in sectors and markets you understand. Ah, the niche argument. Try to invest in places that you are knowledgeable about. For example, you may end up investing in a market that is in severe decline, but you don't know that because you know nothing about the sector. This could all have effects on any stock you may have.

While it is clear that stock trading is not for everyone, the potential that exists within this market is fantastic, and could earn you wonderful rewards in your lifetime.

Chapter 14: Forex Trading

All around the world, we have several different currencies that we use. The US has the dollar, Britain the Pound, and most of Europe uses the Euro. Several other countries and continents have their own currencies as well. None of these currencies really have the same value, as each one is affected differently by factors such as inflation. These factors determine the prices of each currency in relation to another. In the current market, it is possible to take advantage of these factors. This is where Forex trading features. Short for foreign exchange, it is a network of buyers and sellers of currency, who transfer these currencies between each other at an agreed price. If you have ever traveled abroad, you most likely have used forex to exchange currency.

Given that currencies rise and fall in value, we can use this knowledge to earn a profit. Every day, the prices of currencies are moving, which is what is so attractive to most traders. While there is an increased risk, the chance for profits can be very high. Forex trading allows you to bet on how you assume the markets are likely to move. The idea is that you buy a currency pair, when you believe that the base currency will strengthen against its opposite currency. Or you could choose to sell a currency pair if you believe that the base currency is expected to weaken against the opposite currency.

There are several benefits to trading in forex. For one, the market is open 24 hours a day, 5 days a week, from Sunday night when the markets open right up until Friday night when the markets close again. The forex market is extremely volatile, which paves the way for larger profit margins in trading. Forex also provides several risk management tools that you can use to minimize your losses when you need to. These include stop losses, price alerts, running balances and many more. As with the general stock market, you will have a wide variety of optional currencies available for you to trade in. There are over 80 currency pairs that you can choose from; from the major currencies to minor and emerging pairs, all traded in the same place.

While the forex market is seen as higher risk than stocks due to its volatility, it is still the more popular of the two markets, and allows for much greater flexibility in gathering rewards over both the longer and shorter terms.

Trading in Forex

If Forex is the route you wish to undertake, you're going to have to read up on some of the terms and research how the currencies work. Entering a field where you don't understand any of terms being thrown at you will leave you a little bamboozled when you see them. So here are a few that you may see quite often:

Base currency. If you were scratching your head when I mentioned this earlier, then allow me to explain. Base currency is simply the currency that you are currently holding. Usually this is dependent on the country that you are in.

Quote currency. The currency that you will purchase.

Spread. This is the difference between the bidding price and the asking price.

Bidding price. This is the price that your broker is willing to buy your base currency for.

Asking price. This is the price that your broker will ask for when you are buying a quote currency. Once you have learned a few of the terms used, you can do some research on the market without spending the time being entirely confused.

Choosing your broker Once you're getting started, and you know that you want to invest in forex, you will need to find your own broker. Choose a well known and credible brokerage company, as this could have a big difference on your overall future trade success. Look up reviews and info about the best brokerage firms available.

Learn more about the world Research the political spectrums, GPDs, news and trading positions of the countries you are interested in. This will help you find economies with potential growth, and which countries you should potentially stay away from.

Start trading Now that you've got a secure enough knowledge to begin trading, it is time to make your first trade. Choose your currencies, determine the variables and then sit back and let your broker handle the next phases.

Trading Successfully

Once you have started trading and you're familiar with the market, you need to begin honing your skills to make forex trading successful enough to be considered a passive income.

Stick to the plan

One problem that many new traders may feel is the fear of losing. They may buy into a currency, but then choose to opt out if there is a slight turn against them. The key here is to have a plan when you're going in and stick to it.

Set the parameters to ensure you have security in place and then let it run. Only make trades that fall within your plan. It is usually said that you make rational decisions before the trade and irrational decisions after the trade has been made.

Know your limits

Unlike the common gambler, know when enough is enough. Know how much you are willing to take a risk on for each trade, and don't push above them. If you're making a loss, don't begin investing in other currencies in the hope of balancing them. You will lose full control over your trading.

This includes knowing when to stop a trade. Utilize the stop and limit orders you have at your disposal to reach your targets with your trades, or prevent too much decline.

Calculate the success of your system

As a trader, you will need to have a process that you follow with all your trades. However, this should not be followed blindly whether you win or lose. Calculate your success by working out the average success of each trade, as well as the average profit of loss you make from each. While it is important to be consistent in your approach, if that approach is not working, you will need to reevaluate your system and see how you can improve.

Only spend what you can afford to lose

I've mentioned this before, but I'll mention it again to make sure. Do not spend money that you've reserved for household purposes or savings. Only use money that will not harm you in any way, should you lose it. As you are developing this as a passive income, you will need to play the long game, prioritizing stable income over short term reward.

Based on the information above, some would be inclined to think that forex is an easier market to get into, however this is not the case. Your learning curve will be a steep one if you believe that forex can be used as a get rich scheme. Instead, play it slow and you will reap the benefits of your growing experience.

Chapter 15: Swing Trading

As you have gathered, trading can be a highly successful industry for the average passive income seeker. There are several different options to explore to suit your needs and swing trading is one of these. Swing trading has begun to receive an ever growing number of new traders in the market, with more and more people becoming aware of it as an alternative. Day trading is the buying and selling of stocks within a single day. Each day is a new start and nothing carries over. Swing trading is more or less the same thing, however you will hold on to stocks for days to weeks before selling them. Swing trading is a form of active, short term investments (Investinganswers.com, 2019). In more basic terms, swing trading is the act of buying low and selling high.

The premise is that you will buy a stock based on an indicator determining whether there will be an upward or downward trend in the near future. This completely ignores the long term values of stock, prioritizing short term gains. This makes swing trading a high-risk strategy, as because its focus is on the quick stock gains, it is more vulnerable to economic downturns. However, the process for swing training is extensively simplified, meaning you can rely on technical indicators alone when making your trades.

Swing trading is useful to those who have some free time to work around their full time jobs or for students to make some extra cash, as it in no way requires the length of time you would spend on day trading. In general, swing trading will take up approximately 45 minutes of your time. This also gives you time to consider other forms of developing your income. Choosing the right trading platform for you should all be about the personality that you have. Choosing a platform that is against your personality will make you lose the sense of excitement you receive from making trades. Find what caters to your behaviors before jumping on board, so that you are happy with the path you've chosen.

Swing Trading As Income

Investment capital

Although there is no minimum recommended amount, the recommended amount for swing traders to invest is $1,500. This is to ensure that you have sufficient capital to invest in a few trades at the start.

Risk management strategies

Before you get started, as with all trades, you need to limit the amount of risk that comes with the trading. This can be done with a risk management strategy. This will provide an organized and reasonable approach to managing and identifying risks as they come. Being inconsiderate of the risks imposed could be detrimental to your overall stock venture, and could see you stop before you even get started.

What stocks will you trade

One of the things you will need to learn is how to pick the right stocks. Research videos and guides on how to find and pick the right sticks for your needs. Choosing the stock picks is the basis of your swing strategy. Your strategy will be useless if you continue to pick the wrong stocks. A general rule to consider is that large-cap stocks will often have the levels of volume and volatility you need.These stocks will have higher highs and lower lows. Large-cap stocks are the shares of well-known companies that you often see on the news. These companies generally have a market capitalization of more than $5 billion.

Trade in the right markets

To swing trade successfully, you will need to trade in the right markets, at the right times. You will be aware of the fact that there are two market extremes:

Bear market. A bear market is when the stock market is characterized by falling prices and are typically shrouded in negativity.

Bull market. A bull market is the opposite. A bull market shows rising prices and expectations that they will rise even further. Bull markets usually take place when an economy is growing stronger.

Essentially, for you then, you will find that the optimum time to swing trade is in a period when the markets aren't actually heading anywhere. This can be constituted by a repeating pattern in the market.

Consider using a swing trading academy or tutorial to help you practice.

The given saying is that practice makes perfect. A decent academy will run you through the various indicators, alerts and other tools you will need to make your swing trading venture a meaningful one.

Setting Up For the Rewards

One of the aspects of stock trading that is not often mentioned, is the psychology of trading. There is no guide or instruction telling you how to react when things don't go your way, or even for that matter when they are going your way. Knowing how to react to the situation can spell the difference between suffering a substantial loss, or breaking even if it hasn't been a good time in the trades. The idea is not that you need to be fearless. You should fear losing your money. That will make you more careful with it. It is how you choose to combat these feelings and effects with your thinking.

For example, you can **lessen your fear by reducing the risks**. As I said before, everybody's strategy is different, and some may decide to risk more than others. Therefore, you need to determine what works for you, by setting your own limits for yourself and sticking to them.

Although swing trading is considered a form of short term trading; in the world of day trading, it is considered to be a long term trade. As time goes on during these trades, and they start to make a loss for a short period, some investors will begin to panic thinking everything has turned against them. Do not take these losses personally, and instead, **prioritize the long term** profits that you foresaw when you purchased the stock.

Most importantly, in any venture, **never stop learning**. As you journey through, you can end up picking up new skills and techniques that drive you from one income standpoint to the next and so forth, finding ways to get the most out of your investments. Those who stop learning will usually fall behind in the markets, and struggle to keep up with the investors who treat learning their field as a hobby. They love the markets, so they crave to learn more all the time.

The amount of money to be made is entirely dependent on you. Your strategy as a stock investor and the techniques that you use will determine how far your passive income can reach. If it is your first time trading, then swing trading is a great option for beginners to start learning and honing their skills before moving on to more complex forays into the stock market.

Although the hiccup is that you will need a bit of capital, this is to ensure that you stand a greater chance of making a profit in the market, rather than stagnating with a smaller amount. With all this at your disposal, you will find your venture into the stock markets can be quite an interesting and exciting one!

Chapter 16: Personal Brand

Personal branding. I am sure that for many, this is as confusing as it gets. Simply put, your personal brand is how you promote yourself. You are showing off the unique skills and personality that you have for the world to see. In a professional setting, your personal brand is the image that people see of you. It relies on a combination of social media presence, as well as your image in real life. In many ways, personal branding helps to build trust between people.

People are generally more comfortable when they are able to understand what another person's capabilities are. Personal branding helps you to build connections and establish credibility with others. In your area of specialty, having the right connections in the right places helps you to build a reputation, and will improve your ability to gain exposure. Others will see you as an expert in your field and will respect and acknowledge you for it. On a personal note, personal branding can be extremely empowering, helping you to gain confidence and motivation to achieve more.

Yes, yes, I know what you are asking. How does this help you make any passive income? Well, I'm getting there. Personal branding in a more broader term is the process of marketing people and their career as a brand. Well, a personal brand gives you the opportunity to market the products or services you have even further. Think of it this way. If you had a product right now, that you were keen to get on the market, you'd need to attract a customer base. In the case of personal branding, you already have a following who are in tune with what you are offering. Having a personal brand shows what sets you apart from the others within your niche, and shows people who they will potentially be doing business with. Your personal brand streamlines the process it takes to drive your success and takes you even further in the long run.

Creating Your Own Personal Brand

If you want to build your personal brand, you're going to need to understand that you have to put yourself out there; to be seen in the public eye, whether on social media or in reality. People don't do business with companies anymore. They do business with people they like, based on relationships, connections and trust. However, it may still be the early stages for you and we need to start at the basics. Results will also not come straight away. Creating a personal brand will take some time before you start seeing any results. When starting off, there are a few things to consider to get yourself off the ground:

Blogging

Already mentioned earlier, but in the case of personal branding, consider setting up your own blog. Be consistent and blog about topics that are connected to your niche. Share your expertise, and be interactive with the audience members you do pick up to ensure they stick around to learn more about you. Make sure you know who your target customer is before proceeding any further, as this will define who you reach out to.

Guest Posting

Even if you do have your own blog, guest posting can be a great way to gain exposure on more popular platforms. Guest posting is when you are writing an article and publishing it on someone else's website or blog, allowing you to connect with a larger audience. This will help to grow your following, and from there push on to newer ventures.

Host events and be a speaker at conferences

Speaking at conferences, or perhaps even hosting an event can help you to build up your brand in a positive light, and place you and your company in the spotlight. The idea is that you want to use these opportunities to 'sell yourself' to the audience. Show them exactly why you are an expert in your field and know the purpose of your speech. It would help if you had a little understanding of who your audience is as well. This will help you in being able to engage with them. Audience engagement is vital, as this is making sure that your audience is fully tuned in to what you are saying. Think of a magician on stage, and how he shrouds the audience in mystery with his act. You will need to do something similar, using your words and the tools you have at your disposal.

Be active on social media

This is a given in today's world. Make sure that you are active on at least two social networks, and that LinkedIn is one of them to engage with more professional clients. There isn't much excuse for not being active on social media in today's time, and it will result in most people thinking you have something to hide. Even if that is not the case, people will be suspicious of someone who doesn't conform to the set standards. It is not for their interest that you will have social media, but for you to market your personal brand and your business online on the most popular platforms.

The digital world is not the only world

Although most of the ways we have looked at passive income as a whole have been digital, it is not the only way to go about things. As you develop your personal brand, consider potential clients when you are out and about, always keep business cards handy and dress in a professional manner. This will make sure that you're ready to always make a good impression, irrespective of the scenario. The personal brand is you, and so you have reflect that at all times.

Monetizing Your Personal Brand

All of these are ways to develop and enhance your personal brand. Obviously, to begin, you need to have a concept, a plan and an audience you are trying to reach. What we focused on was growing that audience. Now you need to turn a profit off of all this hard work you have been doing. Here you will need to consider the various methods we looked at previous and a few upcoming methods in order to grow your passive income.

Monetize your blog. As a personal brand, you may not want to just litter your blog in ads for profit. Consider courses and ebooks as a way that will further enhance your brand and that you can look to, in order to begin gaining an income.

Create an online community. If you have a sufficient enough audience, you could consider opening up a private community. However, as mentioned, you need to have enough users for this community to be able to run on its own. For this community, you can charge users a monthly subscription for access. If you're unsure if this is a good idea, ask your audience if this is something they would like to see. If there's enough interest then you have a new platform for an audience to communicate and grow from there.

Affiliate marketing. This is something we already know about. Your solid status as a personal brand will help your credibility when marketing products, as your audience are more trusting to what you may recommend. Ensure that the products and services you promote are of the highest quality before you promote them. Promoting and endorsing poor quality products can be detrimental to your brand and the trust the audience has in you.

As you can see, personal branding makes everything rather straightforward when building passive income. If you are consistent in your approach, then you could see your brand soar to completely new heights that you never expected, and revenues will soar with it! (Thimothy, 2019).

Chapter 17: Mobile App Development

In the current age, technology is increasing at an explosive rate. The demand for it is ever increasing as well, with more and more people gaining exposure to the world of technology. This is especially so in the case of smartphones. As we progress, the smartphone is becoming an absolute necessity for anyone living in the modern world.

With this demand for smartphones and handheld devices comes the demand for applications that meet every person's needs. It is estimated that over 5 billion people own a smartphone as of 2019, so it's only natural that this market should be considered for prospective app developers to get their hands into. Even if you're not a developer, you could take the time to learn the trade and consider making your own applications.

The industry ranges from individual developers to developers making applications for large companies. From here, you have the opportunity to involve yourself in an industry that is currently experiencing a growth surge at the moment. If you have a desire to solve problems and some creativity to match, then this is the market you should consider yourself getting into. For current developers, this is a fantastic opportunity to turn your passion into something greater.

Creating Your First App

If you have no prior experience in development, I trust that you know the first step is to get yourself acquainted with the industry. Start learning one of the most popular languages used for mobile, such as Java or Python. Practice creating test apps, or even cloning current ones as practice. Once you feel you're ready to build your first app, we can continue.

Conduct research Check out other apps, and see what sets them apart in the market. Consider their functionalities and what you could incorporate into your own app to make it more successful. Consider the various ways each app makes money on their product, as you will need this information when developing your app later. Search for gaps in the market where there is an opportunity for you to showcase an app.

Don't think big. At first Your first app should be nothing too extravagant. In fact, as you're new, it should be quite basic. This is merely the process of learning what it takes to create your own apps. The only purpose for your app for now, is that it should solve a problem. Why should it solve a problem? There will then be a demand for it. Once there is a demand for it, you can begin to market it.

Research the laws and regulations Before you begin creating your product, make sure it is in line with all laws and regulations related to a mobile application. GDPR (General Data Protection Regulation), AML (Anti Money Laundering) and KYC (Know Your Customer) are all integral with app development, and you will need to be familiar and knowledgeable of all of them if your app is to be successful.

Begin planning your app You should already have an idea of what you plan to create. Now you need to think about what features the app will have and what it will look like. Brainstorm ideas as to the general flow and layout of that. Remember that your app should be visually appealing, and user friendly. You can also plan out how each feature will work on your app, and the processes they will follow. This should include the navigation of certain functions and what will happen if a function is selected.

Start building your app. Once the planning is complete, you will then need to start building your app. To do that, you need the right software and tools. Try to research the best software and tools that will suit your needs. JIRA, GameSalad and Rollbar could be potential app creation software that suits your needs if you aren't too interested in learning to code. However, these are generally very basic, and are usually good enough for the first version of your app, but nothing further. Appy Pie is a potential option if you are keen on writing the code for the app yourself. It all depends on what your needs are and what you aim to achieve.

Test your app Almost every app needs to go through this testing phase. App testing is there to make sure the app works as it should, and there are no bugs or issues that will affect the user experience. Testing will also help you to find ways to make the app even better. You want to be able to develop the best app you possibly can. Pixate and Jasmine are potentially good app testing tools for you to get started with.

Release your app Once all the bugs have been ironed out and everything seems to be in order, you need to place your app somewhere that they can download and install it. The logical choice is with mobile app stores. The two monopolies in the industry being Apple and Google, you're going to want to get your product on their market. So how do we do this? Well, the processes are a bit different.

Google Playstore. Sign up to the Google Play Console and fill out the various details that outline your product. Google charges a one-time fee of $25 in order to create your developer account. Free apps don't cost anything, however Google takes 30% of the revenue for paid apps.

Apple Store. Apple prices are a little different as they charge an annual fee of $99 to all developers. With Apple, you will need to create an iOS distribution provisioning profile and distribution certificate. You can do this through another of Apple's platforms called Xcode. You will also need to set up your tax info as well as sign up for an iTunes Connect account. Once this is all completed, you can then follow the procedure towards adding an app to the store. Your app will then go for review and from there it's out of your hands. For now.

Monetization If your app is a paid product, then you've already monetized your product. However, if you haven't, you need to think about how you are going to do that. With mobile apps, there are several ways you can potentially create revenues towards a passive income:

In-app purchases. One of the many ways is through In-app purchases (IAPs). IAPs are options to purchase an added feature to the app to make it a more enjoyable experience. These generally don't hinder the overall experience of the product, as they are usually just for added visual effects.

Advertising. You could choose to display ads in your apps when users are connected to the internet. These ads can display at certain intervals during the app. If you choose this route, make sure that your app is not overloaded with apps that it ruins the user experience. You will also need to consider what types of ads you will be using (banners, display ads, videos).

Freemium products. These options are quite interesting. The idea is that your product is available for free, however free users will have certain restrictions on their account, that can be unlocked with paid content. This is usually of feature of mobile games, where a user can gain a competitive edge from paying for their content over other users who choose to remain free users.

Merchandise. If you have products that correspond with your app, you can consider advertising these on your app for anyone who would be interested in a potential purpose.

Sponsorship. Although probably the most difficult to attain, sponsorships can be a powerful tool for generating revenue from your app. This method can also benefit developers as they gain exposure to a greater audience.

There are several other ways to monetize your app as well, however the above have generally proven to be the most successful for the majority of app developers.

Marketing And Promotion

Now that your app is complete, you need to build your audience for the app. This will require a bit of work, as app stores have millions of apps and yours is amongst those millions just getting started. Without any sort of marketing, your app will potentially go unnoticed.

One thing you can do to combat this is to ensure that your app has great visuals that draw users to it on the app store. Make sure to include a detailed and interesting description along with a name that sounds catch and exciting.

Consider doing some general advertising of your product. This includes investing in ads on social media, Google and blogs as well.

Once again, another possibility could be for you to start a blog dedicated to your app. This can also provide a great platform for users to communicate with you directly and build an audience for future apps.

Earlier we mentioned that it is okay for the first version of your app to be a very basic version. However, from there, you will need to provide updates that improve the quality of the app and its content. If your app remains the same all the time, people will slowly grow bored and look for something better. It is up to you to make sure your audience remains engaged with your product.

Mobile App Development is most definitely a market where success can take you to the most incredible heights, given its tremendous demand. Even most success can be enough to build you a passive income that allows you to live freely, while performing something that brings you joy!

Chapter 18: YouTube Videos

It stands to reason that if you've not heard of YouTube by now, then it is possible that you've been living under a very big rock for a very long time. A very, very big rock.

In a world where the appeal of easily accessible visual content is becoming ever popular, YouTube has established itself as a mainstay in the market. In fact, YouTube is the largest video sharing platform of them all. YouTube provides an endless variety of content, from documentaries to movie trailers, music videos, educational videos, video blogging (vlogging), original video clips, game footage, live streams and many other aspects that you would like to include. Users on YouTube are allowed to share, like, subscribe and comment on other users as well as add their own videos on the platform. Initially developed by three PayPal employees in 2005, YouTube has gone on to rack up over 1.9 billion users worldwide.

Although YouTube is a free service, it has the option of YouTube Premium. YouTube Premium is a subscription service where users are allowed to enjoy ad-free content, as well as access to exclusive content and offline video playback.

Over the years, anyone from independent users to large corporations have used YouTube to grow their audience base further and attract new members.

In terms of generating income, YouTube and selected creators are allowed to generate advertising income from Google AdSense.

It makes sense right now to potentially jump on the YouTube bandwagon, given the massive spikes in vlogging and demands for online video content in recent times. Finding a niche that isn't already overpopulated may be a little tough, but there is potential even in the most popular markets to be a potential up and comer if you've got something different to add. Even if you are not signing up to YouTube to be a content creator, using the platform to market your current business is perfectly acceptable. Right now, YouTube is where you are most likely to find an audience to attract, as well as the best way to reach younger viewers in the market.

Starting Your Own YouTube Channel

Whether promoting your business or simply wanting to be a content creator, you will have to provide quality content for others to take notice of you. Before that, however, you will need to get the very basics right.

Determine the purpose You're going to need to know why you are creating a channel. Is it to market your business? If you're a content creator, what content do you wish to create? This will all become important later when setting up your account. For potential content creators, remember the importance of a niche and a passion.

On YouTube, you can post videos of just about anything. From video games, to political opinions, vlogs, etc. Whatever is the passion you would like to share, should be what your YouTube channel should be about. Possibly the biggest example of this is PewDiePie. Starting his YouTube channel in 2010, Felix Kjellberg, or PewDiePie, as his username suggests started his YouTube career making videos of himself playing small time indie horror games. Since then, he has gone on to become the most subscribed YouTuber from 2013 up until 2019 where he was overtaken and his channel moved into second place, however still managing to become one of the only channels to reach 100 million subscribers. It all started with a passion...

Create an account The first step you're going to need to make is to create an account. Chances are, you already have one if you have a Google account. However, if you don't set one up so that you can create your own profile on YouTube. One you have a profile, you need to create a channel on YouTube.

Spend time designing your channel, including channel art to share your personality and generate interest in your potential audience. You could choose to upload one of YouTube's templates as your channel art, or upload your own that infuses your energy and interests into the channel.

You can also choose to add a channel trailer. When someone visits our channel, your trailer will help them find out what your channel is about. This video needs to capture the attention of anyone who sees it, and entice them to check out the rest of your channel later on.

The necessary equipment You have your channel set up, but what are you going to use to make videos? At the very least, you will need the basics, which are:

A webcam. Nothing too fancy. A quality high definition webcam will do for now.

Microphone. Preferably opt for a noise canceling microphone that records the audio separately. This will help to prevent any audio discrepancies in the future.

Screen Capture. If you are planning on centering your content around video games or tutorials, you're going to need to invest in screen capture software. There are free options available, such as OBS Studio, that you can use.

Some other equipment to consider is a green screen. If you want to change your background, then you will want to consider investing in a green screen so that this is possible. If you don't have a webcam, and instead you've got a camera or a smartphone, invest in a tripod to hold it stead when you are recording.

Create content Early on, you're going to need some content that people can view on your channel. If you market a channel with no content, this will only frustrate the potential audience. To start, make a couple videos that are of quality content in your chosen niche. Around 10 should be an optimum amount to keep an audience busy in the beginning while you start to upload more content.

Promoting your channel Now that you have some content, you can promote the channel. Remember that promotion is a long term game. You will need to promote your content for a long time before you gain enough popularity to continue your growth without it. So how can you promote yourself?

Social Media. Still the beauty of the modern age. You can reach just about anyone on social media. This will give you a chance to build a small base of followers that will grow over time.

Work with other YouTubers. If you can find other YouTubers who are willing to collaborate with you, this can be a great way to pick up new audience members and expand your networks.

Forums. Forums are where most people go to have discussions and chat about things. Consider searching for a community that is relevant to your content. I would suggest being a member for a little while, and then politely suggesting that you've started a YouTube channel and would like them to check it out. This way, you can build a rapport with them first and from there, you can use this to build a greater procession of followers.

Monetization You are always going to need to find ways to increase your earning potential. Google AdSense will already be available to you, however this should just be an addition to your main source, as the revenue you will generate from AdSense will not be enough for you to have a decent passive income.

Affiliate Marketing will be one of the more popular choices to connect to your YouTube channel. If you've spent some time on YouTube, you'll see how many current YouTubers already use affiliate marketing to monetize their content.

You should also consider **selling merchandise**. As you are now a YouTuber, you will have a lot of people who respect and enjoy the content that you make. Use this opportunity to sell merchandise that is centered around your content, which will help you turn out some substantial products, if you are successful.

Then there is the one that is becoming increasingly popular today. **Become an influencer.** If you are an influencer in a certain niche, you will start being paid to promote anything related to that niche. This can prove a healthy boost to your passive income.

Things You Need To Consider

As an independent YouTuber, you're going to be responsible for all of your own content. This means that you will have to edit your own videos to ensure they are of the best quality. If you have Windows installed, you may already have Windows Movie Maker. If not, consider cost effective alternatives that will match your needs.

You should also plan out your content before you begin. This ensures that you have a reasonable idea beforehand of what you're planning to do, and how it is relevant to your niche. Jumping straight in can leave you disorganized and lost, and you'll have wasted time on a video you most likely won't want to upload.

Pay attention to your viewers. If they leave comments on your videos, try to respond to as many as you can, to show that you are reading their comments, and that you're interested in what they have to say.

However, ignore all the negative comments. Do not engage with any form of negativity that you find. Generally, these are just others who are looking to be nasty, and it would not bode well for your image.

YouTube, overall, is a great platform to share your personality and interests with the world, while potentially generating an income. With it, you can connect with millions of like-minded people who are intrigued by your videos and your personality. Quite frankly, YouTube can be a lot of fun!

Chapter 19: Photography

Photography is one of the great many hobbies that has survived the varying advances of technology. While everyone has gained access to more high quality cameras through smartphones and other devices, there is no substitute for a good picture; taken at the right time, in the right place. I must admit that it is a hobby that I enjoy myself, although I should also admit that I'm not very good at it.

Photography gives us the opportunity to record special moments in people's lives, and allows us to share our experiences in the most meaningful ways. While many hobbies might be inaccessible to some due to a variety of reasons, photography remains an option that is accessible to us all, irrespective of our age or other demographics. Now we have the opportunity to turn that hobby into a passion!

You can use your skills to help others create memorable moments for themselves, with you providing the medium for them to cherish it for a lifetime. On top of that, you'll earn an income!

Creating Your Passive Income With Photography

So let's get started with what you will need first:

A camera.

That's it! All you need is a camera that can take high quality photos to begin with. You can even use your smartphone if it is good enough! So you've got the basics. Where do you start?

Stock photos With the term being fairly self-explanatory, you have the option to sell any stock photos you have. These can be anything from food, to a landscape to a street lamp. This is a fairly easy way to earn a little extra income contributing to the overall value. Stock photos will not make you a lot of money at all, however they don't require much work. You simply have to snap a few photos, and place it on a photography website like Shutterstock. Due to the fairly minimal work involved, adding pictures should be no fuss at all, if it can bring in any sort of income without requiring any of your time.

So if this is not going to generate the needed income, what else can you do?

Courses, Workshops and Teaching Guides A few ways you can supplement your income are with online courses and digital guides. These are considered evergreen products, as they can be sold again and again and will always be available for purchase. So once you've made them, they don't require much invest from you after you've marketed them. Workshops allow you to pass on your practical skills and techniques to those who are willing to learn so that they can better their own prospects.

Selling them as products Now this might make you feel a bit confused. However, photos can be converted and printed onto various products to be sold to the market. Consider printable merchandise such as clothing, postcards, jewelry or even large posters. This can help you determine a variety of ways in which you can potentially sell your products.

Become an affiliate Good old affiliate programs, always coming to the rescue. There are several photography companies, such as Tiny Prints, who will offer you commissions for introducing your audience to their brand.

However. You're going to need an audience.

Start a blog. Use a blog site that focuses on images, such as Tumblr to market your photography skills. Select some of your best photos for display, so that others can see the qualities you possess.

Social Media. Once again, you may want to consider more picture based social media platforms, such as Instagram and Pinterest. The main focus is to attract others to your pictures, and these sites will ensure you pull an audience to your site.

Have a website. Make sure there is a location where others can find you professionally. This can help in the future if you'd like to move on to event bookings as well during the weekends.

Develop a unique photography style. What sets your skills apart from others in the field? Find ways to show off your skills that sets you apart from the competition.

Engage with your audience. Communicate with your audience about your pictures, so that they feel that you are paying attention to them. Be considerate of the opinions they have on your art. Use the opportunity to build a community. This can help gain more traction in your audience growth as more people will want to involve themselves in this ever growing group. That will result in more people seeing your work, and more opportunities to make a profit.

Taking Your Photography Further

Now that you have an audience, a blog, a website and a social media presence, you are in the best position to ensure continuous growth in your photography income. Build your personal brand, and establish yourself as an expert in your field. This will help you in turn with your affiliates, as they will begin to gain more traction due to the increased trust and credibility your audience has placed in you.

If you feel like you've developed your personal brand, as well as your audience to a substantial level, consider approaching lectures and exhibitions to find out if they will display your work.

Out of your main working hours, offer yourself out for portrait shoots with clients and perhaps even events on weekends. While these can be a little tiring, they can be highly profitable and really boost your income further. To be hired in one of these roles, you will need to have a portfolio on your website to ensure that they can view your work.

In your free time, consider entering a few photography contests. These can provide great exposure to your work, and can help you in building connections and bring in more clients. You can also take this opportunity to try and sell your work to magazines. While this may be difficult, it will be a great boost to your reputation and your income.

Photography offers many flexible ways that you can consider to gain an income from your expertise. As a hobby and a secondary profession, it can be highly rewarding, and yet highly pleasurable at the same time.

Chapter 20: Mistakes to Avoid

In general, I've found that the theory of passive income leaves most people scratching their heads. The problem with this, is that once the idea of passive income is explained, their eyes light up with dollar signs and they assume that they are going to be wealthy with these 100% successful methods. I think that's the problem we see in a lot of things these days. People either want it all or nothing at all. However, I wonder if those same people wonder why they stay in medium income employment during the course of their lives, instead of focusing on becoming millionaires and even billionaires. It's definitely a conundrum. I suppose the real reason is fear of the unknown, or unreasonable expectations, which we will look at now. These will be the most general mistakes to avoid when you are looking to develop your own source of passive income.

The Trap of the Mind's Impulse

Strange name to give a subsection. However, it is true, isn't it? That's what happens when we make poor decisions. We react on impulse, emotion and hope, instead of on thought and objectivity. We see this all the time when it comes to passive income:

Nobody has a plan While many will roll their eyes at the thought of planning things out, when it comes to passive income you are going to need a plan to determine what it is you are planning to achieve. Without a plan, you'll lack consideration for the potential costs that may arise, and instead end up digging a hole for yourself.

The Get Rich Quick scheme My favorite. The trap that many find themselves in when they hear about passive income is the belief that passive income will generate rewards in next to no time at all. Setting unrealistic expectations will leave you feeling frustrated and discouraged, and will usually result in abandonment of the trade. Passive income is always going to be a long term game.The rewards over the long term can be substantial but you have to be prepared to be patient, and wait for, then seize opportunities.

Ignoring your assets Throughout this book, I tried to echo that although passive income does not require a lot of work in the long run, the fact is that it is still requires a degree of effort. The reality is that you're still going to have to manage these income streams as long as they are open. If you don't manage them, they may simply fall apart, and you will lose revenue by the bucketload. You need to be aware of the current state of where your income is coming from, and be prepared to act if necessary.

Unknown Finances While it may be a little harsh to say that most people make the mistake of not knowing their finances at all, the fact is that a common mistake is when income and expenses are not tracked. In the case of income, this will mean you have less of an understanding of where your business is going. Is it growing? Are you losing money? You'll have no idea if you've not tracked any income you've received. If you are not tracking your company, you may begin to feel disillusioned with your income, and let it go, even if it was showing signs of growth.

On the other hand, not keeping track of expenses can leave you without an understanding of your cash flow. In some scenarios, you could end up paying for expenses you didn't have to in the first place, however nothing was recorded, and so you ended up increasing your expenditure without knowing it. Being organized will help you in understanding the direction that your business is taking.

Ignoring the effort needed to be put in
Again, I feel the term passive income is being misconstrued. While you need to plan the development of passive income around your schedule, you do need to be consistent with it. If you are decidedly spending a full month working on your passive income, then ignoring it for another 3 months, before starting up on it again, you are merely falling behind, and each time will be like starting your business all over again. Develop a schedule for yourself, and stick to it. Be sure to modify the schedule only when it suits the needs of your business. This will ensure you are still giving your passive income a degree of priority.

Ignoring the importance of research
This is one that I feel can be mentioned for people in all walks of life. I mentioned that you

should have an invested interest in something before you decide to dedicate your time to turning it into a passive income. However, a common mistake we all make is when we believe that we know everything about a subject we are familiar with. There is always something to be learned, and if you head down this path, you could end up making several misinformed decisions along the way that could ruin your business. Always be willing to take on new information.

This should help you in avoiding some of the pitfalls that arise from the development of passive income in the future.

Conclusion

It is always a good idea to keep in your head that passive income is not a source of income that requires no work at all. The unfortunate truth is that it will require a lot of work and dedication in the beginning, but if you begin to think of the long term rewards of your initial hard work, you should be able to continue. That is why the need for passion is so important. It will drive you forward when you feel like it is no longer worth it.

Throughout this book, there have been detailed explanations on several different options to passive income. Some had limitless potential in terms of earnings. Some were very limited in how much they could achieve. However, with all options, you would be perfectly capable of receiving the equivalent of a second salary for the work you have done, provided that you actually put the work in.

It is important to remember that the potential for earnings is just that: potential. It does not mean you will earn that amount, and it certainly doesn't mean that anyone is entitled to that amount, just because they chose the field with the highest potential.

Instead, a form of income with lower potential can be infinitely more successful than one with a higher potential. This is because the practice needs to suit the individual. If it doesn't suit you, it will work against you. Choosing the practice that suits your lifestyle, personality and skills is the best way to earn the greatest profits, as the business will act as a second nature to you.

Remember throughout all of this that the key value is patience. To achieve greatness, you must be prepared to wait. And while you wait, you can learn. This will mean you are using your time valuably, and your learning will benefit the levels of greatness that you hope to achieve.

I hope that you will find the right passive income to suit your needs, and I am sure that with the right ethic, it will be a roaring success!

Good luck on your future adventures!

References

Blockgeeks. (2019). *What is Cryptocurrency? [Everything You Need To Know!].* [online] Available at: https://blockgeeks.com/guides/what-is-cryptocurrency/ [Accessed 14 Dec. 2019].

Crazylister.com. (2019). [online] Available at: https://crazylister.com/blog/dropshipping-success-stories/ [Accessed 14 Dec. 2019].

Edition, F. (2019). *How to Create an Online Course - 5 Steps | Foundr.* [online] Foundr. Available at: https://foundr.com/create-a-online-course [Accessed 14 Dec. 2019].

Investinganswers.com. (2019). *Swing Trading Definition & Example | InvestingAnswers.* [online] Available at: https://investinganswers.com/dictionary/s/swing-trading [Accessed 14 Dec. 2019].

My Accounting Course. (2019). *What is Dividend Investing? - Definition | Meaning | Example.* [online] Available at: https://www.myaccountingcourse.com/accounting-dictionary/dividend-investing [Accessed 14 Dec. 2019].

Ogle, S. (2019). *How to Start Affiliate Marketing for Beginners (A Step by Step Guide).* [online] Location Rebel. Available at: https://www.locationrebel.com/how-to-start-affiliate-marketing/ [Accessed 14 Dec. 2019].

Shopify. (2019). *What Is Dropshipping | How Does Drop Shipping Work?.* [online] Available at: https://www.shopify.co.za/guides/dropshipping/understanding-dropshipping [Accessed 14 Dec. 2019].

Smale, T. (2019). *Guide to Starting a 'Fulfillment by Amazon' Business.* [online] Entrepreneur. Available at:

https://www.entrepreneur.com/article/28227
7 [Accessed 14 Dec. 2019].

The Human Factor. (2019). *The Positive Mindsets Needed For Business Success - The Human Factor*. [online] Available at: https://thehumanfactor.biz/the-positive-mindsets-needed-for-business-success/ [Accessed 14 Dec. 2019].

Thimothy, S. (2019). *Who Are You? Make More Money with Personal Branding | MarketingBitz*. [online] Marketingbitz.com. Available at: https://marketingbitz.com/who-are-you-make-more-money-with-personal-branding/ [Accessed 14 Dec. 2019].

Wanderlust Worker. (2019). *5 Reasons Why Passive Income Is Important - Wanderlust Worker*. [online] Available at: https://www.wanderlustworker.com/5-reasons-why-passive-income-is-important/ [Accessed 14 Dec. 2019].

Written Word Media. (2019). *What is KDP?: Amazon Kindle Direct Publishing Explained - Written Word Media*. [online] Available at: https://www.writtenwordmedia.com/what-is-kdp-amazon-kindle-direct-publishing-explained/ [Accessed 14 Dec. 2019].